FEAR
IS A
CHOICE

FEAR

IS A

CHOICE

Unraveling the Illusion
of Our Separation
from Love

R. JAMES CASE

Front Range Press

DENVER, CO

Front Range Press
frontrangepress@gmail.com

ISBN: 978-1-7352136-0-6 pbk
ISBN: 978-1-7352136-1-3 ebk

Library of Congress Control Number: 2020914867

Editing and book design by Stacey Aaronson

Printed in the United States of America

For Mona, who showed me one side,
and for Michael, who showed me the other

CONTENTS

"There is nothing to fear but fear itself."

—FRANKLIN DELANO ROOSEVELT,
INAUGURAL ADDRESS, 1933

TO MY READERS

I want to be frank with you right from the start so you will know what this book is—and what it is not.

First, you should know that, previous to this experience, I had no design, idea, passion, inclination, or calling to write a book. Not the makings of the quintessential author bio, I know. But the Universe does work in mysterious ways.

For years, I regularly received feedback from my clients that I should write a book. Some actually encouraged me to record our sessions so they could be transcribed. I was touched by the thoughtful expression, but my response remained the same: "I feel no inspiration to write a book, I don't know what I would write a book about, and even the idea of it is not very appealing to me." I would qualify my response by adding that if I *were* to be inspired to do it, I would simply follow my inspiration when the time was right.

And then, that time came. Not in an epiphany or a sudden, irrefutable urge to become an author, but with the inner knowing that something greater was at work. *Why me?* I wondered. *There must be so many more qualified people to write a book like this. People who sit across from Oprah on episodes of* Super Soul Sunday, *or who are otherwise known as experts.* But, as the Universe does when a simple nudge or whisper doesn't motivate us to move toward a life purpose it has in store for us, it began to speak louder to me. Immediately, I was overwhelmed. You see, this book that I had never imagined myself writing began knocking on my soul's door like a persistent visitor. Over the course of several months, all the knowledge, experience, encounters, and inspiration I had accumulated over more than two decades began to flood through me in a series of "downloads." I quickly realized that nothing in my backstory had been for naught; *everything* had crossed my path for a reason. Just like those guests on *Super Soul Sunday*, and those experts whose books I had read or whose seminars I'd attended, I was experiencing a magnificent awakening of purpose, uncovering an as-yet undiscovered gift that was opening a new path for me to help others see something significant from a new perspective.

Which brings me to what this book is *not*.

As I've already said, this book was "delivered" to me in a series of downloads. These stemmed from the numerous books I have read, the many workshops I have attended, the abundance of conversations I've had with sage and enlightened people, and the countless teachers from whom I have absorbed wisdom. Yes, I had professional editorial partners refine those downloads into the book you now hold in your hands, but I did not set out to write an academically oriented book, or even a nonfiction book in the traditional sense. Hence, you won't find footnotes or endnotes, or be stumbling over myriad citations. This is not a sly way of saying that the content within these pages isn't authoritative, or that the sources of it aren't sound. Quite the contrary. It is merely to prepare you for the intentionally structured yet free-flowing reading experience I believe this book was meant to be, in the way it was presented to me. If that sounds a bit "woo-woo" for you, I offer no apology. We must all be true to ourselves in any endeavor, and I believe in my heart that I have been true to the message of this book and its power to spark new ways of thinking about and operating in this glorious gift called life. For the particulars of my sources of influence, I give ample appreciation for my inspiration in the Acknowledgments section of this book, along with a Recommended Reading List that expands upon, supports, or complements what you'll find in these pages.

The overall experience, and what you may gain from it, I leave completely to you.

The Storm

My call to transformation came in 2009, when my life as I knew it completely disintegrated.

Prior to that year, I was traveling every week, working for a company I loved. And in January, a position had opened that enabled me to live and work in the same city, which was something I'd been craving. However, my marriage to my partner of twenty-four years had been tenuous for a few years, and by the end of February, I realized I could no longer continue in our relationship. Despite having once been a synchronistic couple who created a full-scale natural healing center in Arizona, we had become a team who seemed to only create dark clouds and less-than-favorable weather. It took me over a year to arrive at that clarity and summon the courage, but lucky for both of us—though it was fraught with emotion—the separation was quick and undoubtedly a step toward our highest good.

Two weeks later, I was diagnosed with anal cancer.

As I embarked on three months of chemo and radiation, I was thrust into an extraordinary journey into Self. I began breaking down my relationship with and understanding of fear, and as I did, I discovered I was no longer in reaction to my life—and that this was only the beginning of this part of my journey.

After I completed the treatment, I was excited to return to work—only to be terminated by my boss, who, ironically, had been in treatment himself for colon cancer. Needless to say, I was nonplussed by his decision, particularly when I believed—erroneously—that he could relate perfectly to what I had been going through. Then, three months later, I lost the home I had owned for over twelve years as a casualty of the housing and economic crash.

As you might be thinking, I wasn't kidding when I said my life completely disintegrated.

While this was by no means the first of many challenges I'd experienced as a child and a young man, what had begun to feel like a degree of welcome self-exploration during the cancer treatment morphed quickly into a massive storm brewing inside of me. It felt as though all the conditioning of my upbringing, my teachers, and my family were conspiring to keep me in my sameness, to drink from a river of history that would perpetuate the "reality" of fear that had worked overtime to fill me with illusions of unworthiness, powerlessness, self-doubt, blame, and self-sabotage.

As this internal storm strengthened, my primary thought was, *I need to get Home.* Somehow, in the midst of the chaos, I understood that "Home" for me was alignment with my authentic self, not someone else's idea of who I should be. Yet as the winds of change and transformation swirled, pounded, and pulsed, rattling me to my very core, I was terrified of what aligning with my true self would actually mean. Suddenly, though I longed for that transformed version of me, I pictured myself pulling on the door of an imaginary storm shelter and seeking safety inside. There, I would be protected from the raging conflict and confusion that was surrounding me, from the enveloping debris of my current life. But that imaginary door wouldn't open for me. *Was it locked or stuck?* I wondered.

I banged on that door in my mind, feeling incredibly alone. I was taunted with thoughts of failure, of weakness, and of caving to what I mistakenly believed was the easiest path. The thoughts were so loud and so powerful that I felt they would completely overwhelm me. Tears streamed down my face as I begged and bartered, yearning to be rid of the despair that was consuming me.

I was feeling so deeply, so viscerally, I decided that all I could do in that moment was let go. To allow it all. To stand in the center of what I created and surrender, to just be *with* it, instead of *in* it—which was the one thing I hadn't done. Then, in a seeming "moment of mercy" from the Universe, a new feeling began growing in my chest as I sat with this experience, and my mind began to clear and focus. It was a feeling of potential, of possibility. As I began to allow it, it became stronger and clearer, and

I felt new determination rise up in me. I wasn't sure precisely where it came from. I only knew that my thoughts seemed brighter and clearer than before, more expansive than the "me" I usually listened to. And as this clarity "spoke" to me from inside, I became grounded in its focus: forcing myself inside that shelter would mean remaining who I was.

It was at that moment that I consciously decided to "release" that storm door and change direction toward the door of my "Home," the one that represented my authentic Self—the Self that had been striving to be set free for decades. That door wasn't far away, but it required a change of perspective to get to. And the storm didn't simply subside when I made the decision to change my perspective; in fact, it almost seemed to rage more intensely, determined to keep me afraid and scattered. Yet I allowed the winds to continue whipping around me without offering any resistance, completely focused in my new perspective, despite not knowing what "Home" would truly feel like.

When I arrived at the door of my sacred space, my Home, the storm began unraveling itself, losing its focus and intensity because I was no longer attending to its energy. I was exhausted, but the clarity was profound. Part of me just wanted to sleep, to go unconscious, to simply disconnect. It was comforting to know that I could do that now in peace, that I could truly rest in this new perspective and "space" of consciousness.

I know it all sounds terribly dramatic, but that's how storms are generated. I had truly arrived at a crossroads of deciding to stay stuck in sameness or to strive for expansion. I can honestly say that once I summoned the courage to choose expansion, it launched one of the most extraordinary and magical times of my life. I began to see, in rich detail, the choices I made and didn't make, and I was able to internalize how my choices created my reality—every single bit of it. The best part was the inner knowing that I could go forward, consciously choosing what my new path would be. I was poised to rise from my own ashes and begin my transformation. In reality, I had just transformed my *entire* experience, and now I was actually beginning the process of integrating that profound new perspective and energy.

The components that comprised that enormous transformation inspired the writing of the book you now hold in your hands.

And so, as you embark on this journey with me, I ask that you set your conditioning aside for a time and approach the coming chapters with willingness and openness. You will know truth when you experience it, and when you experience it you will be filled in ways you've always craved. You will likely be challenged in your viewpoint, perspective, and beliefs—as was I—and that's a good thing. Allow it and see where it takes you. When you enable that part of you—the one that designed this life experience—to fully engage in these pages, you will wake up to all of who you are, and that will create transformation unlike anything you have ever experienced.

PART I

THE FOUNDATION OF BELIEF

CHAPTER ONE

Our Relationship with Fear

ear. Simply using the word can create a powerful response in people. It has become a tool for manipulation in marketing, politics, news, media, schools, jobs, careers, and more. We create acronyms in an effort to make it less impactful, such as False Evidence Appearing Real. We encourage people to embrace and/or confront their fears with idioms like "Just do it" and "Push through." We have even created holidays that perpetuate fearful events and times in history, like "Never Forget 911" and "Holocaust Remembrance Day." It seems that fear is everywhere and something we merely have to accept in our experience in order to live on this planet. In fact, there apparently isn't much NOT to fear anymore: climate change, viruses, war, starvation, natural disasters, political elections, food and water contamination, weather, your neighbor, guns, cops, people who embrace a religion different from yours, people of different races . . . the list goes on. Every day there is some new study, research, or opinion on the newest, most pressing thing we need to fear. The results?

They're catastrophic.

Sorry, I couldn't resist.

See how easy it was to trigger a response?

The truth is, very few people will read that first paragraph and not have a fear-based response. Why is that?

Using fear as a weapon or tool is certainly not new. It has been going on since the beginning of our species, at least according to research and history. Fear is engrained in us day after day, year after year; as a result, fear-based information is wired in our brains, and most often these thoughts are remembered more readily than happy thoughts. There is also confusion created in our psyche and energy by the over-stimulation of fear, because the fear reaction and the survival instinct are not the same, and do not provide the same function. Because of this, we start believing that having fear means our survival is threatened, and that is simply not real or true.

Even in the Bible, the translation of the adventures of Adam and Eve introduce us to an angry, vengeful God who was so disappointed in the weakness of his creation (us), that all these millennia later we still have the "fear of God" within us. During the various periods when the Bible was translated, those in power knew that if they could keep the masses in fear, they could control them. Hence, the proliferation of terms like, "Beware God's wrath!" (More on this in Chapter Three.)

Today, we have moved into whole new territory with

fear. Manipulation of people through fear has become an art, tapping into our subconscious experiences and using it to influence us to think, buy, and act in highly specific ways. Companies spend millions—even billions—of dollars on fear manipulation because, nearly without fail, it works. Sounds pretty daunting, doesn't it? Perhaps the most baffling part is that so many people are completely aware that this mind-play goes on, yet quietly go about their business believing there is nothing to be done, or believing it simply "is what it is." I propose that the reason this happens is because we are looking at the phenomenon of cause and effect backward. We'll get more into that later on.

Lest you think I'm trying to scare you by telling you these things, I want to be clear that my goal is simply to bring awareness. I am not on a mission to bash anyone or anything, but rather to WAKE YOU UP to your power and potential regarding this "illusion"—which is that we have come to believe that fear is a real thing instead of a feeling we ourselves control.

Let's face it: We use fear as our excuse for everything. We swim in it, we indulge in it, we wallow in it, all the while believing it is something with great power and control over us—not the other way around—because that's what we've been trained to internalize.

Believe it or not, having fear as the basis of your experience is not natural. Instead, it is the source of so much that is not working in each of our lives—from relationships, to success, to health, to jobs, to creating the life you want, to having what you want. We are truly meant to thrive in this human experience, yet we've largely settled for surviving, possibly with a half-hearted smile and taking a stab at feeling grateful. HUH?!

It is time to wake up to the illusion that is fear. It is time to recognize and change this entity that has become for so many the basis of their existence—some in big ways, some in smaller ways. As we take this journey together, we are going to dive deeply into the construction of fear, dispel the illusion of "the man behind the curtain" (who is real by the way), and look squarely at the reality that, ultimately, *fear is a choice.*

My relationship to fear changed dramatically when I dove, head first, into a program called Higher Brain Living®. This extraordinary process activates and stimulates the prefrontal cortex of our brain. For those who are not aware, the prefrontal cortex is the center for joy, passion, creativity, high-level problem solving, and thinking. The process enables people to radically shift state—which means we can change our current experience, situation, feelings, or beliefs in a profound way. In doing so, we achieve states similar to those that meditating monks have worked decades to achieve. It is truly incredible. These results have been consistently demonstrated through EEG studies, and they are currently being researched at the University of Iowa.

With Higher Brain Living, I developed the tools that allowed me to shift from experiencing the world through the primitive "lizard" brain, to living in consciousness, or in a world of opportunity. What does that mean? For me it meant no longer being run by fear. I am now able to see every situation in my life as opportunity. From this perspective, I am able to access solutions and ideas that were not available to me in the shut-down, fear-driven state. It's like having a view from 50,000 feet above my life with the perspective, freedom, and passion to explore opportunity after opportunity, and then apply this perspective to all areas of my life. The result?

Transformation. Powerful, all-encompassing, extraordinary transformation.

Until I experienced this shift of state, I'd only read about this level of awareness, and I assumed I'd never experience it myself because I couldn't see myself sitting under a tree meditating six or more hours a day for decades—which is what I had read many times throughout my journey about achieving this state. You can imagine the thrill I experienced when I discovered I didn't have to do it that way, that that higher-level awareness and freedom was available to me without living in a remote cave and becoming a monk. Even more exciting is that it's not a fleeting or one-time thing: this transformation continues to unfold to this day. It is a remarkable journey filled with the kind of peace, passion, purpose, and connection I know every human on this planet dreams about.

And it's all because I now understand that fear is a choice over which I have complete control.

I'll be honest: the shift out of the fear bubble is an interesting and eye-opening one. While it seems like having no fear would be awesome, and it is, it is also challenging. To help explain this better, let's clarify a few ideas.

The first idea is about *beliefs*, which by very simple definition are simply thoughts that you keep thinking. Beliefs are typically constructed as a result of an emotional experience that had an impact. For instance, imagine a child is playing with a red ball in the front yard. At some point, he throws the red ball into the air to catch it and misses. The ball bounces and rolls out into the street. The child runs into the street after the ball and gets hit by a car. Though he survives, one of the potential beliefs he develops is an inordinate fear or dislike of anything red. His subconscious builds this experience because red balls are now associated with something life threatening and dangerous. Out of this frightening experience, the child forms a new belief—and this could be just one of many from one individual incident. The thought that he keeps thinking involves seeing the red ball and then feeling fear, pain, unconsciousness, anxiety, or all of the above. Basically, the experience leaves a mark, and that mark becomes a belief. The beliefs built from that one event could carry through that child's life all the way into adulthood.

Now imagine this experience on a larger scale—for

instance, at the family level. There are beliefs formed and transmitted within our family structure. Many of these beliefs carry on generation after generation, becoming part of the unconscious fabric of the family group's life experience.

Now go even bigger. Beliefs are built at every level of the human experience. They grow from individual, to family, then to community. From community they develop into cultural beliefs. From cultural beliefs they spread to territorial. And from territorial they become continental, and finally global. When these beliefs reach a global level, they are considered "mass consciousness," which is nothing more than mutually agreed upon thoughts that everyone keeps thinking. (More on this in Chapter Five.)

The first and biggest challenge to understanding beliefs is recognizing them. But remember that beliefs are built on habitual thinking. When a belief is so powerful that it becomes a part of mass consciousness, it takes time and conscious effort to disengage from it. This disengagement occurs when you "shift state," or raise your vibration.

It is important to understand you will never destroy, remove, or eradicate your beliefs. You can only transform them, which in simple terms means taking all of your previous understanding or experience with you as you transcend your beliefs—or elevate yourself through the above-mentioned shift state or vibrational change—into a new understanding or experience. Ultimately, everything is energy. Fear vibrates at the low end of the spectrum, while love/joy vibrates at the high end. By engaging a vibrational shift in your energy, you can begin building a new approach to that area of your life, one that comes from the most authentic part of yourself.

The easiest way to start this process—which expressly involves detaching from fear—is to question why you do what you do. Take any aspect of your life—your morning routine, the purchases you make, the clothes you buy, the way you raise your children, or even how you brush your teeth—and begin to observe what you do, and then gently inquire why you do it that way. Once you see for yourself all the beliefs that structure your decision-making process, you can begin to ask, "How would [insert your name here] do this? How would [insert your name here] want to do this? How would [insert your name here] do this in a way that brings [insert your name here] joy, or peace, or calm, or satisfaction?"

You may ask, "Why am I using my name in these questions in the third person?" The answer is straightforward. Doing so objectifies your experience. In other words, it engages your mind and your consciousness in an *objective* way, enabling you to bypass much of the mind confusion and chatter that comes from engaging the questions *subjectively* when you think in the first person using "I" or "me." Overall, it allows for a deeper clarity that doesn't engage resistance from your trained history.

Here's what this might look like, taking clothing choices as an example:

Q: How would Jim dress?

A: Fairly conservatively.

Q: Why?

A: Because Jim's dad always dressed that way and said it is how successful people dress (belief)

Q: How would Jim want to dress?

A: With more creativity, color, and comfort.

Q: How would Jim dress in a way that brings Jim more joy?

A: Taking a risk with more color and comfort and not shying away from innovative style choices.

This is a fairly simple example, but see how quickly it elicits Jim's true desire?

As you perform this exercise, notice the feelings that arise and begin to define *your* particular experience uncluttered by the noise of "have to," "supposed to," and "it's always been this way." One thing I can say with absolute certainty is that *nothing* has ever always been the way it is claimed to be.

As you embark on this journey of self-exploration, you may notice that you encounter fear. If so, internalize that it is a *feeling* generated by the part of yourself that is content with maintaining sameness. Now, observe it as an *object* in your awareness. You will see that the "fear" is not *you*; it is merely an element you have control over, the same way you have control over the way you conduct your morning routine, the way you dress, etc. As you shift this perspective, you will become clearer and less willing to engage with the feeling of fear. When that occurs, you will encounter one of the most powerful states in consciousness. I call it the state of "Not Know," a beautiful and awe-inspiring state that allows for all possibility.

In "Not Know," you are in a void state. Since your consciousness (and the Universe) abhors a vacuum, your consciousness, not your mind, will begin to expand in new directions, allowing you to explore potentials and possibilities—all of which exist in you right now, but are kept at bay by the mind that wants to keep you locked into "the way it has always been" because ultimately, to the mind, same-ness equals safety/survival. This happens because to your mind—and only to your mind—that fear has stimulated a strong belief in lack of safety. In other words, fear acts as a mask, or block to the "Not Know," greatly limiting your own potential, *but only in your mind.*

My hope, as you read this book, is that you begin to unravel this illusion of fear in your life, and to recognize that we have been *trained* to fear the life we are here to create. Knowing this, I'm eager for you to begin to put together the pieces of your personal fear story, see them for the illusion they are, and finally liberate yourself from the fear experience that has undoubtedly kept you from living the full and actualized life you came here to live.

But before we do that, let's take a short journey through evolution to see how and when fear came into being.

CHAPTER TWO

How Fear Staked Its Claim in Our Collective Psyche

You may have heard it told that early man was a more instinctual being than he was a feeling or thinking being. His experiences were that of an advanced mammal with some rudimentary cognitive skills that slowly evolved into discovering other skills, like communication, fire-building, tool-making, etc. As these skills began to increase in quantity and complexity, more and more of the brain had to be engaged. As these new skills and their accompanying knowledge created new neuropathways of learning, the capacity to learn grew—and in turn created changes in the physiology of the brain and the body, moving the entire being into a forward progression of evolution that has continued for millennia.

When man experienced and took notice of things that he could not readily understand—mostly natural events such as lightning, thunder, tornadoes, hurricanes, volcanos, and earthquakes—his brain and body developed new responses. The human capacity for understanding had not yet evolved enough to explain and comprehend these experiences; during the more instinctual period in our distant past, these events were simply responded to, with action taken in an attempt to ensure survival. As deeper cognitive functioning evolved, so did the desire to understand and explain what was being experienced. And so these early people began to interpret, create stories, and imagine reasons for these events, even though their thought process was still based on limited or no understanding. What's more, while a desire grew to understand the experience of life around him, man's desire to understand himself was also evolving. He began to ask himself: How could these events be happening? What do they mean? Who or what is doing these things?

Because humans have an innate desire to understand their experiences, and to give those experiences meaning and purpose, these early humans began to create meaning as a way of understanding these strange and often scary events. How did they do this? By making up stories using their imagination. Over time, these intricate stories became the fabric of their lives and experiences; they told them repeatedly until they became the core beliefs of their experience, passed on generation after generation. It wasn't until their cognitive abilities evolved again that later humans were able to explore, test, experiment with, and understand these experiences in two distinct ways.

These new and different ways were called *religion* and *science*. Religion was born of the ritual, superstition, and magical thinking developed over millennia of stories; and science came from experimentation, the trial-and-error processes that man devised in an attempt to more concretely explain his existence.

The purpose of understanding all this evolution is to allow us to clearly see that our first experiences with the emotion of fear came from encountering things we could not explain. It was decided (or agreed) that there must be some force(s) much greater than us, and that apparently this force didn't like us, and would even kill us, given the chance. And from this belief that we were not safe in the world under the invisible control of a mighty and terrible power, we gave birth to mythology and fear. As a result, our very survival was no longer limited by what our senses could identify for us, i.e., animals, plants, and the terrain—and now there was an even bigger, unknown element: the gods. You might even say that fear is the "original sin," that point when humanity determined that it was separate from God. This concept of separation triggered a convoluted and difficult journey, and it created the fertile, rich soil on which fear could grow like a weed—and along with it our sense of unworthiness.

Once a baseline of fear was established in the species, propagated by stories of things way beyond our control and understanding, this message of fear and unworthiness grew and deepened in our psyche. Those in power began to realize that if they could claim to be closer to God (or the gods) than the rest of humanity, they would retain ultimate power and control. And so to integrate this belief of even further separateness, they began to use their power to threaten the survival of those less powerful, continually stimulating the flight/fight response of the people they were attempting to control. This constant assault on survival stimulated and embedded the fear response in the consciousness of the masses. And as we see that everything is in constant evolution, the embodiment and transference of this provoked fear evolved as well. Fear became part of the belief structure of entire cultures, deeply embedded in the consciousness and psyches of virtually every known society across the globe. Stories of fear were told and retold, sometimes with a heightened overlay of fear. As these beliefs were passed on life to life, generation to generation, more and more people were swept into a lifestyle based on fear, wherein they not only believed in the fear, but developed powerful belief systems that one's very survival depended on maintaining a focus on fear.

And so, over thousands of years, fear and stories of fear became part of our DNA—our very cellular memory. This is significant on numerous levels when you understand that our DNA is an incredible database. Within this amazing part of human physiology is everything we are, ever were, and ever will be—as individuals, as a species, and as a life form. It has been proven through science that within our physical structure is the same material that stars are made of. Pretty miraculous! When you consider all of that potential (both "good" and "bad") that lies dormant within all of us, it is unfathomable. In addition, when you consider concepts like The Hundredth Monkey—a hypothetical phenomenon in which a new behavior or idea is said to spread rapidly by unexplained means from one group to all related groups once a critical number of members of one group exhibit the new behavior or acknowledge the new idea—you begin to get a glimpse of our interconnectedness to EVERYTHING. This understanding is critical to understanding the evolution of fear.

Consider, too, that when anything within a *culture* becomes pervasive, it becomes part of the fabric, or DNA, of that culture as well. Since no system, race, culture, community, or individual exists in a vacuum, all of the significant pieces of potential that become woven into this fabric called DNA is shared. Put simply, as we explored and discovered more and more of the planet, more and more connections were made between different tribes and cultures—and this enabled more and more expansion as various DNA co-mingled, expanding all of that DNA potential like never before. Since fear and separation are not, and were not, something exclusive to any group of people, each sought ways to express it, explore it, and understand it within the context of their own cultural system. Within all of them, fear evolved into a tool of control, manipulation, and power manifested through this foundational logic: If the gods can wield their powers over all human beings, and I can convince people I come from gods (bloodlines), then I can also wield that power over others.

It is also important to note here that humans as a species seek connection. In whatever circumstances, there is a deep desire to be part of a tribe. It is as critical to survival, and maybe even more so, than food. Hence, if you can wield enough influence and power to make people believe you can remove them from their tribe, it triggers the already deeply held belief in one's separation from God/the Universe/Source. In short, when you can keep people stimulated in an awareness of separation, you can keep them in fear. And this level of fear is not your run-of-the-mill type. This is *core* fear, the kind that can be completely irrational and illogical, born from the belief—and illusion—of separation.

And there is another piece to this equation.

Within early populations, there were different levels of consciousness, just as there exists now. Every tribe had its chief, but it also had its shaman, its seer, its mystic. Later, these magicians became rulers and priests, people who were believed to have "special" and direct connections to God, or the gods. This reinforced the belief of separation within the masses, which created even greater fear built on the feelings of worthiness born out of the belief in separation.

Are you seeing how this experience is not new or much different from the experiences of our current reality? It has simply evolved and become embedded in the fabric of our now collective world.

By now you are probably thinking, "This is fascinating, but how does this demonstrate that fear is a choice, though it appears to be tied to our very physiology?" Excellent question! And here is the answer.

First, we must accept the concept that fear is/was not intrinsic, it is/was learned. The consciousness of fear has been handed down, trained and retrained, over and over and over again. And as with anything we learn, we have the choice to use it or not, to engage it or not. As such, while fear has become a deeply embedded societal belief, it is still a *learned* response. Remember: beliefs are simply thoughts you keep thinking. The more consistent the thought, the deeper and stronger the belief grows.

A powerful tradition that supports these beliefs can been seen in virtually all cultures, tribes, and religions—and that tradition is storytelling. All of a culture's shamans, seers, priests, and rulers found ways to document their stories of fear by creating books, bibles, holy works, and tombs that continue to perpetuate stories from generation to generation. And regardless of the incredible nature or forced believability of these stories, the simple act of repeatedly telling them created entrenched "beliefs" that worked their way through the generations. What anchors people to continue to believe them—for no other reason than survival, and believing their very existence depends on it—is, you guessed it: fear. The incredible part of this is that we will believe the unbelievable if it means our survival is at stake. In other words, we are willing to suspend logic and rationality *because* of that fear. And much of that is due to our deeply engrained concept—and frequently misguided conditioning—of what the majority of us call God.

CHAPTER THREE

Exploring an Understanding of God

The question, "What is your relationship with God?" conjures a multitude of answers, thoughts, and reactions from most people—and that is good. I believe that our answers to this question express the core beliefs that govern our lives. That may seem like a pretty bold statement, but if you think about it, every aspect of your operating belief system has its foundation in your answer to this question. Before we talk about how and why, however, let's clear up something so this exercise in self-reflection doesn't get derailed by any confusion or misunderstanding.

First and foremost, "What is your relationship with God?" is NOT a religious question; in fact, it has absolutely nothing to do with organized religion. The question may stimulate all of your religious concepts and beliefs, but the question itself is not religiously motivated. To understand how this is possible, let's look at what religion actually is.

According to the Oxford English Dictionary, religion is defined as: "the belief in and worship of a superhuman controlling power; a particular system of faith and worship." In other words, organized religion is the structured framework we use to express our version of spirituality. Virtually all organized religions are founded on a core belief that there is an entity greater than us, and that we pay homage to and worship that being for our continued well-being. That's part one.

The second part of organized religion is the dogma, or the set of principles laid down by an "authority" that deem them incontrovertibly true. Entire structures have been created to define how worship should be orchestrated in order to gain the attention of the entity that many call God; throughout history, there have been endless examples of these organizations and how they operated. But the important thing to understand about organized religions is that they are, without any dispute, completely created by man. *Completely*. If this throws your foundational beliefs into a spiral, remember that I invited you in the Introduction to be open to having your beliefs challenged. Remember, too, that the intention of this book is to create awareness—that fear is indeed a choice, yes, but also of the components that make that statement true. In the case of religion, there are definitely aspects we must look at objectively to understand just how much fear plays a role.

In every religion there are stories, fables, gospels, etc.,

that were all written and rewritten and updated and rewritten . . . by Man. This is not conjecture. All religions are run by humans, organized by humans, implemented by humans, and governed by humans, with their writings translated into texts, bibles, and holy books by humans. In other words, they are man's interpretation and reinterpretation of ancient events overlaid and mixed together.

While we are all free and welcome to believe whatever works for us, there must be a clear understanding that organized religions were developed as a means to control and manage people by stimulating a core belief of unworthiness, infusing it with tremendous amounts of fear, and wrapping it up with a pretty ribbon called "love." Yes, there are many great truths laced in and throughout organized religions, but they have become distorted by man's faulty interpretations—and those interpretations are largely based in fear.

Please don't let this offend you; this is not in any way about bashing religion or spirituality. The purpose of putting this explanation forth is to bring understanding to a foundational part of our existence—a foundation that is NOT religion but is still what we call God.

Now, let's return to the question I posed at the start of this chapter. While it's not a religious question, your answer may be very religious, or it may be more metaphysical and spiritual in nature. As such, in an effort to remove the emotional charge that is created within organized religions with relation to the word "God," we often replace it in today's society with more generic, less provoking words, such as the Universe, All That Is, The Great I Am, Om, Source, or whatever allows you to enjoy and enhance your spirituality outside the confines and regulations of religion. (I will use "God" and "Self" as well as certain of these names interchangeably throughout the book, all of which denote my reference to an infinite intelligence that creates all things.)

What is vital to realize here is that the question "What is your relationship with God?" is highly personal. It speaks to the very core of who you are. Regardless of your human beliefs, your relationship with God reflects the deepest aspects of the entirety of your being. Indeed, this is the ultimate existential question, crucial to our understanding and evolution.

While Christians have long discussed and awaited the "second coming" of Jesus, I would like you to consider the true "second coming" as the realization that God is already here, living and breathing through us, in us, and as us, and by us actualizing and aligning with that great truth. Coming to this alignment with who we are is *not* a religious experience but rather a deeply personal and spiritual one.

The experience of being in alignment is unique and beautiful for every single being. There is no right or wrong way, no protocol, no measuring stick of worthiness. YOU are already that and more! Living in alignment is about turning away from being outwardly driven and fear moti-vated, to being inwardly driven and allowing your awe-someness to express through the powerful inspiration created through your alignment with Self/God. This is how heaven on earth is created right here, right now. And it happens individually, whenever *you* are ready. In other words, heaven on earth will not happen in a surprise visit, in some nebulous future, when some angry god decides. It is in the NOW that you decide. It's all about alignment and connection with the Love that is All That Is.

So, as you approach this profoundly personal question about your relationship with God, it is important you understand that your responses will be layered and complex. You may need to allow your answer(s) to steep for a while as you peel back the layers to fully grasp their significance. Every aspect of your feeling and thinking about this question reflects an aspect of the conscious/ unconscious structure that molds your beliefs, behaviors, and ideas. You must be willing to drill down into each aspect to allow yourself to fully understand the construction of your consciousness.

I know this sounds huge, and it is, but there is no need to feel overwhelmed. If you do, I want you to begin to observe the feeling of overwhelm as merely a defense mechanism employed by the subconscious mind to keep you from upsetting the status quo of your life, and to keep you safe in the world. Here is where you can use your breath to change your vibrational perspective. As you breathe yourself into this new perspective, you will begin to experience the fear (or any emotion really) that will become an "object" in the field of your awareness. You will also begin to realize it has no real bearing on you, except for the energy or attention you put on it. You can even say, "Thank you, subconscious mind, for trying to protect us, but we are safe. We are navigating this a different way now."

Once you establish that *you* are in charge of how you feel, you must be willing to put everything on the table to effectively answer the question about what your relationship with God is. You must be willing to look directly into the answers and see them for what they are. Some answers will likely come forth immediately and resonate with the teachings you have received through schools, churches, parents, etc. And yet these "pretty" and "well-accepted" answers are typically only the first layer. They are the answers that make us look and feel religious or spiritual according to what we have been taught is right and good. But as you go beyond these answers, you may be surprised how much lies beneath—and how much of that is seemingly contradictory to those surface answers. This is not only perfectly okay and normal, but it is necessary if you want to fully embrace the question, and more importantly, your true self. You'll see that delving deeper and deeper into this question will bring up deeper and deeper feelings that may prove quite uncomfortable, but ultimately, they will prove liberating and relieving.

Here is an example of intentionally asking the same question over and over to push the person to go deeper, striving to arrive at a level of profound insight. Note the heightening of emotion, which is common in these types of sessions.

"What is your relationship with God?"

God is everywhere! She is in all things. I experience Her in the blades of grass, in the trees, in the sun and in the breeze ..."

"What is your relationship with God?"

It is all Good! Everything is good and everything is God.

"What is your relationship with God?"

Wow! I feel that you're being really intense right now. I'm an empath, so I can feel everything, and your energy is making me uncomfortable. So much anger in your second chakra.

"What is your relationship with God?"

I feel like you're really coming from Ego right now. Why are you judging me? Please don't try to psychoanalyze me. I will not talk to your Ego.

"What is your relationship with God?"

crying This conversation hurts my heart so much. Please stop being so cruel! I can't believe you're doing this to me. I'm feeling so much anger with you right now. Please just go. I need my space.

"What is your relationship with God?"

[Without any words the answer comes through physical demonstration as collapsing into a puddle of dark emotion, pain, despair, and anger.]

This step-by-step process of digging into real answers is a powerful example of how we build and sustain a hollow belief structure, one that is created to cover up or protect a deep sense of unworthiness. It is also used to smooth over a cesspool of negative emotions directed at the Self that are often too big to even look at. In other words, this sense of unworthiness feels so powerfully bad that, in a Wonder Woman–like way, a person may feel the need to put up a shield or wear protective wrist bands to help deflect energy seeking to penetrate their space. In the case of the above example, every response to the question was a deflection. When this occurs with someone, they don't assume even minimal responsibility for their experience, specifically because that hollow belief structure is so firmly planted that it keeps them from truly looking at how they experience and feel about their own self. However, if they continue to drill down, they are likely to make great progress toward understanding their current lack of connection and alignment with God. Put simply, when the façade is removed, true healing can take place.

Here is another example, using a drill-down method:

"What is your relationship with God?"

God is my creator.

"So, what is your relationship with God?"

I am created in God's image.

"Okay. But what is your relationship with God?"

What's written in the Bible.

"What is your relationship with God?"

That God made Adam and Eve and we are all descendants of them. So I, too, am a creation of God.

"Great! So then, what is your relationship with God?"

I am his creation.

"And what is your relationship with God?"

I try to listen to my Creator. I try to do what he says.

"What is your relationship with God?"

It's written in the Bible to love one another. I try to follow the Ten Commandments.

"And what is your relationship with God?"

I don't know. I think I do the right things. I try hard to listen and obey his commandments, but I'm human. I am flawed. I'm working my way back into God's grace because I am unworthy.

Do you see how this person just identified a few core beliefs he has about himself, from which he operates every single day of his life? *I am unworthy. I am flawed. I am not in Grace. My human-ness means I am less than. It is difficult to hear God. I struggle to follow God's commands.*

Do you have any of these same answers or feelings?

If so, take these statements of unworthiness and drill down into each one to gain deeper understanding of the structure of your beliefs. Simply being conscious of these underlying messages is powerful and life changing.

Here's another example.

"What is your relationship with God?"
I don't like to use that word.

"Okay. What is your relationship with God?"
It makes me uncomfortable.

"So, what is your *relationship* with God?"
I just don't like how using the word "God" feels.

"Okay. *What* is your relationship with God?"
Awkward. Uncomfortable. I feel like I want to cry.

"What is your relationship with God?"
I don't have one.

Do you see how simple questions are all that is required to arrive at answers? In this example, another core belief is uncovered, that of feeling completely separate from God and having no connection whatsoever.

In these scenarios, keep in mind that there is normally a wide range of emotions during the interchange that are not detailed in words. Note that regardless of the response or emotion, you want to continue to ask the same question, possibly shifting the emphasis of different words, until you *feel* your "truth'"emerge. Every time I asked a question of the person I was interviewing, it created a deep emotional response. Note these responses in yourself as you go through this exercise, as they are extremely important in helping you better understand where to place your attention. Particularly notice any feelings of inadequacy, fear, unworthiness, sadness, anger, pain, separation, etc. Now, consider that these feelings represent what has been called our "Emotional Guidance System." We will focus on this topic exclusively in Chapter Twelve, but for now, it's important you know what this signifies is that our emotions help us to understand where our true alignment, or core vibration is. Here's what I mean.

When a question stimulates a negative emotional response, that response is an opportunity to understand that you are out of alignment with the Truth of who you are. In other words, negative emotions are clear messages that you and God/Higher Self/the Universe are not looking at the question or situation from the same perspective. In other words, your "rational" perspective is rubbing against or resisting the greater perspective regarding whatever you are dealing with. This "rub" we experience as negative emotion. The degree of your divergence from that greater perspective will determine the depth of your negative emotion. To further clarify this, consider that God is you and you are God. When you experience negative emotional tension, it is specifically because you (self) are in conflict with You (Self). As such, the intensity of your negative thought or feeling is in direct proportion to the distance your thoughts and/or feelings are from your true alignment, or your Source/God.

I realize that this is a profound concept, so let's address another part of this.

You have likely been raised to believe that you and God are separate or different. So to hear "God is you and you are God" might feel odd, or even sacrilegious. But I'm here to tell you that is true only in your thoughts and beliefs about who you are. When we talk about being in alignment, it refers to how much or how little you accept or do not accept that you and God are one and the same. The tension created within the self (human) all stems from this lack of alignment with Self (God), which is the energetic experience of separation—or better, the separation of self from Self.

Another way to think of it is this: if you try to separate your arm from your body, there will be great pain. As you start to pull on your arm to separate it, you feel discomfort. If you continue to pull harder, you will create even greater discomfort and ultimately tremendous pain. When you attempt to separate an organic part of yourself from yourself, it does not feel good. And so if we understand and accept that God is you and you are God, any thoughts and feelings that do not align with this sense of one-ness will cause discomfort and pain, i.e., negative emotions and feelings. Knowing this, you can use the newfound awareness of your Emotional Guidance System consciously when answering the question to allow yourself to gain the greatest clarity.

"What is your relationship with God?"

There is no God.

"What is your relationship with God?"

God is a man-made concept to deal with the fear of death and dying. The only thing that is real is what we perceive with our five senses, period. The rest of it is hogwash. Science explains that when we die, that's it. We are gone, annihilated. What was once my physical body will turn to dust.

"So, what is your relationship with God?"

I have relationships with real people. I have relationships with my family and friends. I do not have a relationship with some imaginary being in the sky.

"What is your relationship with God?"

Nothing else exists unless science proves it otherwise. I live my life to its fullest and I try to stay really healthy because I only get one chance ... so I'm going to try and get a whole lot in before I die.

"What is your relationship with God?"

This question and conversation are pointless. I do not believe in your God.

"What is your relationship with God?"

If and when there is scientific proof of the existence of this so-called God, I will entertain your question. Currently there is no such scientific proof. So I guess if I were to answer, I would have to say there is no God at this time.

In this final example, we find a core belief that there is no God, the implications of which can be staggering to one's well-being. Yet, make no mistake: it is actually impossible in any reality for there to be no relationship with God, or Source.

Using the previous analogy of removing a body part, even if you actually cut off your arm, it does not change the reality that your arm exists in physical form; and by cutting the arm off, you are only hurting and destroying YOU. It is the same when you believe that you have no relationship with God. What you are actually saying is that you (self) have no relationship or connection to yourself (Self). Can you see this is a literal impossibility? If we return to the "rub" we talked about a little earlier, it's clear that this belief would create a big one! While this rub feels a bit more "stuck" than the first one I mentioned, rest assured that with attention and intention to gain clarity through the question, you will find resolution, and eventually release yourself from that rub.

The belief that there is no God is probably the trickiest type of response to unravel. When there is such conviction in a lack of scientific "evidence" that proves God exists, the arguments become "God proofed." In other words, the intellect so rules the consciousness that there is no room or avenue yet created to connect to a greater perspective or experience.

One can start by looking at any single element of our miraculous human body to experience "proof", or validation of something much greater than ourselves: the way our cells and organs function completely defies human logic; same goes for the proliferation of nature, for the way the Earth rotates around the sun at precisely the right distance, for how gravity keeps everything—even our vast oceans—anchored to our planet, just to name a few. So why do some people insist that there is no God?

While this may sound surprising, it is not uncommon for this core belief to be based in a deep-seated fear of death—or to be adopted after powerful and impressionable life experiences have already occurred. Some possibilities are the early death of a parent or parents, a powerful empathy within that focuses on the pain and suffering a person observes, or possibly experiencing great pain and suffering oneself. When tremendously painful events like this occur, a person often chooses what seems to be a "safer" position of belief, one that denies that part of Self that cannot be "proven", or the part that cannot resolve an apparent untenable perspective.

Remember that each and every one of us came into this life the same way, and we have all moved through the various stages of human development. Yet, at some point, a person with this type of experience may determine that the world is a random, painful place of suffering. Frequently, this viewpoint grows out of experiences during early development that causes powerful conflict between the input from the five senses and a person's innate and deep sensitivities. The core belief based on these traumatic events develops as, "How can there be a God that allows so much pain, suffering, death, and destruction? Why would an all-powerful being allow that?" So, these conflicted individuals develop a strong belief to make the most of what appears to be a purely human science experiment, relying solely upon what can be proven and created strictly from human abilities. The beliefs here, when drilled down, are built completely on the illusion of rationality, along with the apparent inability to come to terms with early irrational and unexplainable experiences and impressions. In short, the person seeks to answer the ultimate spiritual question: "What is real?"

The profundity of the question, "What is your relationship with God?" and, more importantly, the answers, will lead you unfailingly to the truth of your experience in your human form and within your human consciousness. I have made the examples short for purposes of demonstration, but yours may prove to be much longer. If you find your mind resisting and jumping all over the place in an effort to not let go of your deeply entrenched teachings, simply be persistent. You can also do this exercise with a trusted person who can assist you in really drilling down. You may also be best served if you do this as a writing exercise; putting it down on paper will get the ideas out of your head so your mind cannot create confusion—which, sadly, is usually a distracting defense response to protect the status quo.

If you are willing to devote the time to meditate on this question, and to understand all of the potential answers, you will go far toward your own enlightenment and exponential growth. Expect that this exercise will take you some time—days, weeks, even months, depending on how engrained your beliefs are. Also expect that as you consciously dive in to the question, you will activate your consciousness in a whole new way so that your discoveries will lead to even more revelations and clarity.

One note of caution as you do this exercise: do not allow yourself to get hung up on any one thought or emotion. If you have a complicated relationship with a divine Creator, or no relationship at all, this process will stimulate your consciousness very deeply. Allow that. You will have aha moments. You may notice changes in your dreams. You may find yourself feeling vulnerable or reactive. Do not fixate. Keep moving forward. Once these beliefs become conscious and are no longer hidden, you will have the ability to assess, change, or replace them. This is achieved because you are no longer unconsciously holding on to prior beliefs that kept you feeling unworthy and separate. Instead you are allowing yourself to operate your life from better feelings and ideas. For example, if you believe that you have no relationship with God—meaning that you have no relationship with Self—

you can immediately begin to change it by doing those things that demonstrate there *is* a relationship. You can use meditation, prayer, writing, or whatever activity inspires you to connect even deeper with your Self. In doing so, you will find no validation in the existing belief of *no relationship* because you are actively building a powerful new dialog and relationship with Self, one you can begin to allow because YOU are having an internal experience of YOU. In this shift you recognize that there is no call or need to place your power or well-being outside of Self/God. By exploring the practices that work best for YOU, you can reach and keep your alignment—and you can find your way to knowing God . . . I mean, You!

Once you have gone through this transformational exercise of redefining your relationship with God/Self, ask yourself what it feels like to recognize yourself as God. If that wording is a stretch, then go back and do the exercise again. There is an amazing quote from Marianne Williamson that says, "Our deepest fear is not that we are inadequate. Our deepest fear is that we are powerful beyond measure." In other words, we are never broken, only misdirected or poorly focused.

The ultimate challenge in these questions is this: in order to recognize ourselves as God, or in complete oneness with God, we must disengage from our externally developed focus, or rather, that God exists *outside* of us, *separate* from us—a focus that was developed through the environment in which we grew up, *not* within spiritual reality.

CHAPTER FOUR

Taking On the Energy of Our Environment

From the very beginning of our human experience, we are learning, adapting, aligning, and evolving. At the moment of conception, we begin to imprint the emotional experiences and energies of our parents, striving to find alignment within the energy field of our host. In short, we are in the process of active evolution, of becoming and radically transforming within the context of time and space.

A powerful part of our evolution occurs during the transition from being *outside* of time and space to existing *within* time and space. In other words, we find a "safe" transition pocket within the womb that allows us to evolve and grow as a physical being. While powerfully and directly connected to our Source via an energetic "cord" that we are never separated from, we are also connected to our physical mother through the umbilical cord, taking in the predominant energies that surround and flow through us via her physical, emotional, mental, and spiritual experiences.

During this phase of our evolution as a developing fetus, we are still deeply connected to God, to our Source, and we are still predominantly energy as our physical vehicle grows. This incredible vehicle is itself evolving and adapting to the flow of new energy, building chains of data, experience, and potential via DNA, all of which come together to create the most successful environment possible for our physical adventure.

Most of the experience within the womb is limited to the *feeling* wavelength, meaning that we are experiencers first. You could also say that we are "BE-ers"—we are deeply and acutely aware of what we experience, though all of it is feeling. These experiences begin to imprint on our consciousness, and they set the stage for our emergence from the womb into the vast playground of time and space to continue our evolution as a physical being.

While this early human development is fascinating, you may be asking, "Why is this important to understanding how fear is a choice?" *Because fear does not exist anywhere in the consciousness of this newly evolved being until it is introduced, in the womb, by the fetus's host.* In short, any powerful emotional experiences the mother has during pregnancy are imprinted on the growing fetus's consciousness and may be activated later on our journey as we become more actively conscious in our experience. More on this soon.

Once we are ready to leave the womb and enter the world as a physical being, we continue to be powerfully connected to God and Source. In fact, for the first few months or so, we are more aligned *there* than *here*. Think of this period as allowing our physical vehicle to adapt to our inflowing consciousness, and our consciousness to anchor in the physical vessel, as well as adjusting and adapting to the external stimulation of this new physical reality we have entered. This period of adaptation allows the inflowing consciousness to inform, and begin to guide, the physical experiences of our life.

At this stage of infancy, we remain actively in the "BE-ing" state—fully engaged in feeling, sensing, and experiencing this new physical reality—with our evaluating criteria based solely on two significant elements: Love and the absence of Love. Let me be clear: *everything* infants experience falls within this spectrum. (We will continue to utilize this evaluation process throughout our adult life, though we will learn to assign more complexity and mass-consciousness distinctions to our adult evaluations.)

As our physical vehicle acclimates itself to the environment, we begin to absorb information and experience through our five senses—and as we indulge in all of these experiences, we are imprinting, feeling, and assessing "Is this Love or the absence of Love?" There is no judgment in this process; it is all pure experience layering itself into our being. We also begin to recognize one of the first laws of physical reality: cause and effect. For example, we are hungry, we cry, someone does or doesn't respond with food; we are startled, we cry, someone does or doesn't soothe us. We also become physically aware of desire. As we are loved, comforted, sung to, read to, etc., we take in the positive feelings of those bonding moments and crave more of them. We also begin the process of conscious assimilation and understanding that we call learning. In other words, our development shifts focus from purely experiential/sensory experiences and events and becomes directed more toward developing the mind in accordance with the mass-consciousness perspective of human development.

Prior to our attention being directed to developing the mind, everything we learned began as a conscious experience in the womb, as a particular vibration that caused excitation within the field of the fetus's awareness. As the brain developed, these events became experiences that were catalogued by the conscious and subconscious, building neuropathways in the brain. Good or bad, these experiences became part of our subconscious mind—the part that drives our conscious experience.

Now, as a little "BE-ing" in the physical world, we are a sponge to everything and anything that we can engage. We are still deeply and energetically connected to our mother, but she is no longer a "filter" for us as she was when we were in utero; any powerful emotion that is aimed specifically toward us bypasses any potential filters or screens and imprints directly. This is important to understand because it dramatically impacts our consciousness, but more importantly it impacts our *sub*conscious. Let's break this down for a bit more clarity.

All information and experience occurring in our physical reality comes through the five senses. When there is a strong energetic or emotional impact event, it is imprinted, as a part of the survival mechanism, or reptilian brain. The effect of these events is then "stored" for future reference, as well as to ensure our continued survival. As a result, these events also deeply impact our development going forward. Understand here that the subconscious *does not differentiate between positive and negative*—these are subjective assessments left to the *conscious* mind. The subconscious is more like an endless warehouse of data storage with no judgment, no qualification.

So, in a child's physical reality, her first instinctual response to a forceful negative command is felt as a response to the *energy* of the command. Because the energy is usually intense—either out of fear, anger, or both—the energy directed and expressed by the parent causes a deep feeling response in the child, stimulating a powerful desire to "understand" what has happened. Since her cognitive functions are in development, the child can only gain a rudimentary, and generally faulty, understanding of her experience. And so, left with no alternative, she makes up reasons for the issue, connecting her own dots in her very limited imagination. This is called a "primitive cognitive impulse," the first of many levels of experience in the evolution of a child's cognitive development. (Infants will go through each aspect of the human evolutionary development periods as they grow into childhood, young adulthood and puberty, early adulthood and adulthood. This is a powerful topic unto itself and is explored later.) The dots children connect become part of their subconscious database. Some of these events will have a powerful impact on their future experience, while others not so much.

Here is an example.

Your child is exploring her world, grabbing and touching virtually everything. As she reaches for an expensive and potentially breakable object, or something that could be dangerous, your response is an intense "Don't touch that!" Though unable to register your words, the child experiences your energy, which is "louder" than your spoken words. Having been engrossed in her moment of exploration, the energy of your command jars and frightens her, evoking an immediate emotional response. Keep in mind that the child's response is to your *energy*, not the command. As soon as this momentary shock passes, her curiosity about that object of her attention, despite your response, remains her focus.

When the child continues to grab for whatever that object is, the energy of your response tends to grow larger and more intense. And yet, strangely enough, the child often continues in the quest to fulfill her curiosity. (How many times have you seen a child reach for a mother's shiny earring, seemingly endlessly, even when directed away from it repeatedly?) If the end result of the parental guidance is corporal punishment of some kind, the child's experience of the parental energy goes from merely seeing it, feeling it, and hearing it to experiencing it as physical; the smack on the hand, the swat on the butt, grabbing, pulling, or shaking now add a profound and potentially negative experience into the child's consciousness, and a new *belief* very likely begins forming. This belief becomes: "When I do this it feels amazing and I am loved," or "When I do this it feels awful and I am not loved."

I said earlier that as our physical vehicle begins to acclimate itself to the environment, we begin to absorb information and experience through our five senses; imprinting, feeling, and assessing "Is this Love or the absence of Love?" As children begin to learn language, this is still true, but their minds become engaged in a new way. In other words, in the early months of life, the child takes in a parent's negative response, but as the parent's energy dissipates, so does the child's attention to it. Once there is active focus on learning and language, however, these energetic events take on a new dimension. So, when a child experiences physical repercussions *along with* the negative energy of the parent(s), it creates an impact event. These impact events are what stimulate decisions in the developing child. These decisions are not rational, but rather based in self-preservation. Again, the child intuits some form of, "When I do this it feels amazing and I am loved," or "When I do this it feels awful and I am not loved."

And this is how and when fear begins to take hold in a child's psyche.

During pregnancy, if the mother was consistently in fear, it is likely that the child developed an internal experience that was restricted or contracted, mirroring the conditions created by the mother's physiological response to the fear she was feeling. When that same child, as an infant or toddler, experiences that fear feeling emanating from the parent—whether expressed as the parent's own fear, or the feeling of fear invoked in the child by the parent's harsh tone or action—the child's cognitive function now engages and "meaning" is ascribed to this energy. That "meaning" becomes a cause-and-effect experience that gets stored in the subconscious.

More often than not, these cause-and-effect associations hold little or no logic—yet these experiences become the foundation of something critical: belief building and the fear response. What this means is, going forward, the child will associate anything close to that experience with that *specific* event, determining that there is negativity, anger, pain, etc., that must be avoided. The inner child's simplistic reasoning says, "If I do that again, then Mom/Dad will do that thing that makes me feel really awful about myself." It is important to take note here of the child's reasoning and language: the child is not responding to whatever *action* the parent said not to do; the child is responding to the *effect* it created in the parent in the form of anger, violence, frustration, or any level of negative energy. (As children get older, reasoning skills develop more fully and responses become more complex, but it is not unusual for them to grow up avoiding desires or activities similar to an early negative experience, because their subconscious association now fears that the outcome will be similar to the result of that experience.)

What's crucial to understand through all of this is that although the memory of being non-physical is still a strong part of a young child's life, the child interprets a parent's negative response as being the result of a flaw in the child's own perfection, or Love state. And it is here where the fear response is taken further. This feeling of being responsible for a parent's discord happens because the child has no other context available to "understand" the intense negative energy coming at them. Said another way, in order to manage the impulses and desires that appear to create a negative response in their parent, the child develops a fear response. This fear response quickly becomes integrated into the subconscious and becomes part of the child's basic survival instinct. Once this fear response is integrated, it becomes the default setting going forward—and this is where fear becomes an integral part of the child's repertoire (and the adult he becomes), and ultimately a choice, unconscious or otherwise.

This alone would be enough to create inner conflict, but what makes it even more challenging is the addition of two significant elements: the influence of *subjective "realities"* and of *mass consciousness*, both of which we will explore in the next chapter.

CHAPTER FIVE

The Influence of Subjective "Realities" and Mass Consciousness

As a child develops and becomes more and more immersed in the physical time and space experience, the strength of his/her connection to God/Source does not change. What does change is where their attention is focused. Because the immediacy of stimulus and response is too strong to ignore, children have no choice but to become consumed by the experiences of their physical reality. As you can imagine, while there is a strong pull toward following their internal guidance system, the noise of the physical world begins to get louder. As children interact more and more, their attention—and intention—develops in alignment with what they can touch, taste, see, hear, smell, and feel.

All of our senses filter through the lower brain, or the fight-or-flight mechanism. This part of the brain has the responsibility of ensuring our safety and survival.

Remember how we talked about cause and effect in the last chapter? This is the Law of the Universe that has a child enraptured during his early developmental stage. Through exploration of which events cause certain results to occur, he is attempting to fully experience this amazing and stimulating world. But as his cognitive awareness grows and develops, another shift occurs, moving him into the world of understanding. It is here that things become complex and confusing.

Why is that?

Because the process of understanding is predominately *subjective*, not *objective*.

Subjective understanding—or what I call subjective "realities"—is accepting a new belief because we are *told* to in some form or fashion. As a child, we may be told that performing a certain religious ritual is the only way to gain favor with God, or that if we aren't "good," Santa Claus won't come. *Objective* understanding, on the other hand, is achieved through our own experience. Early in life, this kind of understanding can come about from things like knowing that when we touch a hot stove, we get burned, or if we fall down on asphalt, it hurts and can result in a scrape.

Objective understanding may vary in certain circumstances (falling won't always result in a wound, etc.), but overall, the lessons are fairly solid and unwavering. With subjective understanding, however, not only does it vary based on one's family beliefs and the influence of others' beliefs on our own, it is also affected by a construct of physical reality we briefly touched on earlier called "mass consciousness."

Mass consciousness can be described as a type of collective agreement on the nature of reality. It is the result of billions of people thinking the same thought, creating a belief about it, and then determining that their collective creation is reality. The problem is, much of what exists within the mass consciousness is simply made up. Many of the universally believed ideas about life, or beliefs that we carry about our world and how it works, are simply ideas formed by powerful people who are able to disseminate their ideas repeatedly and powerfully until the belief takes hold. After that, the belief takes on its own life, becoming "the way" certain things are thought of, executed, or done.

The result is that people become embedded in the personal and group consciousness and are manipulated, driven, and continually triggered into an emotional response by it. This is the basis of how marketing any product is done—and this is the illusion that has a powerful grip on most every human being who has yet to awaken.

An example of this can be found in the societal fable that was woven around the concept of the engagement ring. You may—or may not—be surprised to learn that the engagement ring never existed prior to it being promoted in an ad campaign by a diamond brokerage company named DeBeers. DeBeers proved so effective in its campaign that the engagement ring became an integral part of societal norm and marriage ritual across almost every country and society. It is now so completely embedded in mass consciousness that it is unthinkable, and dare I say unacceptable, for a proposal to not include a ridiculously expensive ring that has absolutely nothing to do with the relationship or marriage. How do you think that was accomplished? You guessed it. *Fear.* DeBeers created fear in women by suggesting that she needed appropriate investment in a ring to legitimize the commitment of the man. And DeBeers created fear in men that without an appropriate investment in a ring, he would not be worthy of the woman of his dreams.

Allow this to settle into your consciousness.

We see similar collective beliefs when it comes to how we view our country's history. In many ways, this is also a subjective "reality." We've taken in information presented through a particular lens intended to create specific understanding—according, that is, to whomever presents the information. Textbooks are largely subjective, for example. Historical events are chosen—or not—to build a landscape of history; certain people are highlighted—or not—to present the desired picture of what occurred. Because of this, we tend to all learn basically the same "facts" in mainstream schools, and then go through life believing what we've been taught as the truth of our history. This, too, is a form of mass consciousness: moving through life with a common belief that is likely not the whole truth, or sometimes not true at all.

For a child, subjective beliefs begin to creep in early through various means: family influence, the media, cartoons, religion, peer pressure, etc., all of which affects the child's internal guidance system. Further, as parents and other influential adults reinforce mass-consciousness concepts, they mold the child's own consciousness in profound ways. In other words, what was once a natural, easily flowing exploration of this physical world now becomes lessons fraught with angst, anxiety, and fear due to complicated nuances in teachings governed by the ongoing debate of right vs. wrong.

Much of the confusion we experience dealing with the mass consciousness of child rearing is that it is not connected and aligned with Truth; it is instead connected to and aligned with resistance to Truth. Is it a wonder that parents today are so conflicted and confused? As you can imagine, a child's physical reality continues to pull him deeper and deeper into "illusions" supported by the energies of his parents and the mass-consciousness beliefs surrounding him. These energies are not only distracting from the child's internal guidance system—which is always centered in well-being and authenticity from our connection with the Divine—but they forcefully guide the child to focus and believe in ways that, to the child, frequently feel unnatural. Some examples of this could be forcing a child to dress a certain way or play only with certain kinds of toys according to gender norms, or to have a specific type of hairstyle, or to adhere to particular religious or cultural practices, or to only be allowed to participate in certain activities, play a specific instrument, or engage in particular sports because of perceived norms or parental desires.

As these expectations are driven into the child's day-to-day existence, the child's focus becomes more and more outwardly directed, meaning they begin to put more importance and credence on what's happening *outside* of themselves, and begin disengaging from what is happening *inside* themselves—which often has to do with desiring a feeling of approval. Because, in most cases, parents don't encourage or guide children to be inwardly directed (such as creating a practice of deep breathing with their child, or setting aside quiet time for them to daydream and use their imagination, or asking them to follow their heart when given a choice of activities), they begin to either lose touch with or discredit their internal experience. This is because they are told and shown by the world around them that an internal sense of alignment is less important than gaining approval from the outside. Though children may maintain a strong connection to and interaction with their interior world, their environment and the majority of people in it continue to call them to focus outwardly.

The closest many children ever get to encouragement toward focusing internally is when they are brought into religion. Unfortunately, the ideas, concepts, and beliefs typically support the illusions of an angry God watching the child's every move, creating a sense of unworthiness and powerlessness, based in fear. Through these religious teachings, along with those of parents, teachers, and society, the habit of fear becomes firmly embedded in the child's consciousness.

Now, you may be asking, "How can any parent avoid raising a child with some level of this kind of conditioning?" And the answer is this.

I realize it may seem like it's almost impossible to raise a child with a strong connection to his or her inner guidance system, or connection to Source, in today's society, without some dogma or unhealthy conditioning creeping in. Even if *you* give your child every opportunity to live authentically, there is still the outside influence of others—whether through subjective "realities" or mass consciousness, both of which can require a great deal of self-confidence and not caring what others think to go against. However, it is important to understand that this exposure is not all negative for a child; these stages and teachings are also crucial and necessary for growth. Remember, too, that a child specifically *chooses* her parents and the environment for her journey, specifically because she knows that the combination will provide the perfect opportunity for her greatest evolution and growth of her Soul. This can be tough to grasp when we consider some of the situations children are born into, but it is here that we must remember that greater forces are at work than we as humans can fully understand in our physical bodies. (More on this in Chapter Fourteen.)

The bigger message here, for right now, is creating *awareness* in you that subjective "realities" and mass consciousness have a massive influence on how children take in their beliefs—and consequently create a level of fear surrounding those beliefs. Not conforming—if the importance of conforming and believing as others believe is the primary message a child receives—becomes cause for fear.

Whether you're a parent or not, as an adult reading this book, my hope is that you're able to connect some dots to your own anchors to fear—*not* in a blaming way or that renders you a victim, but to unravel some of your own conditioning so that you can not only move forward with heightened awareness, but take steps toward dissipating the ways you've interpreted fear—erroneously—as necessary in your physical journey.

PART II

THE ENGRAINED
AND ACCEPTED ROLES
FEAR PLAYS

CHAPTER SIX

Physiology and Fear

S omeone mugs you on the street. A car speeds toward you in the crosswalk. A snake appears alongside a path you're walking. All of these situations activate a remarkable response in the human body—one that is focused on keeping you safe and alive in the face of threatening circumstances.

This physiology is brilliant, to say the least. A complex processing system—called the sympathetic nervous system—exists below the conscious threshold, at the heart of which is the oldest part of our brain, commonly known as the "Lizard Brain," survival brain, or lower brain. It includes the amygdala, which is associated with the "fight or flight" mechanism. A bit further down, in the brain stem, we also possess the "freeze" response—when neither fight or flight best serves us in the moment—to help us remain motionless while developing a survival plan.

To use current technology to promote understanding of this: if you have a smartphone or computer of any kind, there is an operating system "in the background" that is continually processing, refreshing, storing, and routing data through the nervous system of the computer or phone. Millions of processes go on below the surface, keeping resources and data moving to the right places at the right time, all of which come together to ensure maximum efficiency. There are also safeguards in place to prevent viruses, attacks, and corruption from reaching the essential data. This background processing runs 24/7 without any attention to it. When something is encountered that might be a threat to the system, the computer sends up a warning notification with a brief description of the impending problem. This gives you, the user, an opportunity to correct the problem and prevent any damage from occurring to your computer's system. It is pretty amazing technology; if we don't click on a bad website or link, or in some other fashion leave ourselves vulnerable to attack, the system will generally operate pretty smoothly.

Think of your physical body in the same manner.

The survival brain is at the core of the physical operation, and our five senses function as a filtering system, continually taking in data. This data is processed by the survival brain as our "first line of defense": input is assessed for any threat to survival, and should a threat be detected, a command is issued to the brain to implement appropriate protective measures. The body then initiates a complex array of chemical, neurological, and physical processes, which prompts the body to release chemicals to stimulate elevated awareness, as well as to increase physical capacity and deliver an immediate "message" to shut down, avoid, or evade the detected threat, whatever it may be.

As I mentioned, there are three options available when the survival response is triggered: fight, flight, or freeze. However, one of the misconceptions about these options is that none of them is actually the *primary* response. Yes, the body automatically engages this process for the goal of protection and survival, but there is actually another response that comes first.

When the sympathetic nervous system is engaged in self-preservation, biology and chemistry come together synergistically to create a "superhuman" state. Every system shifts into high alert, instinctively filling the body with adrenalin and other chemicals to increase the body's physical ability to respond quickly. This is important to remember because the fight, flight, or freeze experience comes *after* the initial "superhuman" response. In other words, this superhuman response offers immediate clarity about the threat and *then* informs the next choice of fight, flight, or freeze.

Interestingly, this automatic process is not associated with *emotions* but rather with *ancient instinct*; when an event is truly life threatening, all actions are instinctual. Myriad stories describe people being able to sense solutions, spring into action, and execute incredible physical acts that could only come from a superhuman place. None of these feats could be achieved under "normal" circumstances, or rather, in a state of being unaltered by that instinctual response.

What's perhaps most surprising about this super-human experience is the absence of fear. What this means is that we aren't actually reacting because we're afraid; we're reacting from hardwiring that protects our-selves from harm or death. It is only when the superhu-man instinctual response subsides that our mind and emotions get involved. This is critical because it clearly demonstrates how fear is not inherent in the response, and therefore, we can begin to understand how fear is a choice.

Let's look at another aspect of physiology in relation to fear that shows us how much control we actually have. Quantum physics tells us that *everything* is vibration, and that *everything* vibrates at a certain frequency. Each thought and each emotion that we focus on carries its own particular vibration, which affects our physical body. For example, joy has a high vibration and carries low density or weight, while fear is a low vibration that carries high density and weight. When you develop alignment with higher vibrational energies—happier, more joyful energies—your being becomes less dense and heavy. As such, you can consciously *change your vibra-tion* so that your energy vibrates above or outside the vibration of fear, ideally at the level of happiness and joy, and therefore alter your body's physiological expression.

Let's explore how a person can accomplish this.

You've no doubt heard people say, "I feel weighed down with these feelings." This statement speaks directly to their vibrational impact. You can assess this pretty easily within your own experience by simply stopping for a moment when you experience an emotion and feel what's happening in your body. You will feel either a sense of rising or lifting, or a sense of falling or pressure, or something along that continuum. You will also notice as you continue to experience the feeling that your body will feel lighter, stronger, and more alive, or denser, heavier, and weighted down.

If you're having a difficult time discerning precisely what you're feeling, try performing the following two exercises.

First, remember a time you felt fear, maybe about speaking up, or job performance, or politics, or health. Something you can easily identify as a feeling you experienced. Recall the details of that time and for a moment allow yourself to re-experience the feeling. After you've done that for thirty seconds to a minute, observe the specific sensations in your body. You may feel a heaviness in the pit of your stomach, or a clenching or shutting-down feeling. Particularly notice the feeling of gravity pulling you down, slowing you down, or giving you a feeling of heaviness.

Now do the same exercise with an experience you would consider one of the best days of your life. Re-create it in your mind. See all the details. Now observe the specific sensations you're feeling. What are some of the words you would use to describe them? Empowered? Loved? Uplifted? My personal favorite word that encapsulates a positive feeling is "invincible." Now, bring your awareness again to your body. Do you notice a lightness, or a relaxed feeling? Maybe a sense of peace?

Take a moment to reflect on the profound differences between the fear and the joy experiences you've just conjured. Now take a moment to reflect that YOU, consciously, just *created* both of those experiences. (Note that this proposes that maybe fear, and all emotions, are actually a choice.)

Now, take in that what you have done is identify *vibration.* You may not have been aware of it before, but you are engaging your vibration at all times, simply by what you put your attention on. The wonderful thing about this awareness is that becoming conscious of your vibration gives you the ability and power to choose what vibrations you want to experience. Becoming conscious also means you have the ability and power to *change* that vibration.

There are numerous ways this vibrational change can be accomplished, and a multitude of powerful tools are available to assist the vibrational shift. Some general methods include meditation, yoga, listening to uplifting music or to recordings of teachers who elevate you, writing in a gratitude journal, being with positive people who inspire you, engaging in prayer, etc. On a more extreme scale, a person might take the path of becoming the student of a Master, living and studying in an ashram, or even becoming a monk.

Whatever means you choose, you must find something that allows you to shift your state from one that resides in some level of fear (such as lack, worry, anxiety, doom and gloom thinking, frustration, dwelling on the past, anger, etc.) to one that raises your vibration to Love (such as appreciation, relaxation, security, abundance, excitement, creativity, allowing, etc.). The more you consciously engage these vibrations, the less you will feel the vibrations of the opposite feelings. Step into the exercise below and see how powerful it is. Even if you are going through a difficult time, there are still countless things, feelings, experiences—and even difficulty—that you can appreciate, if you make the *decision* to consciously do so.

Here is a powerful exercise of expressing appreciation, or as some call it a "rampage of appreciation." You can do this exercise anytime and anywhere, even while doing something as routine as using the bathroom. It is amazing how much appreciation you can muster for something you normally consider mundane, or take completely for granted.

Here's how it might sound as you go (with an important note to focus on as many of the details and steps of the activity as you are able. Appreciate it ALL!):

> I appreciate my amazing body for letting me
> know what it needs . . . I appreciate my
> connection to my body and willingness to

listen to the prompts I receive from it . . . I
appreciate that I can walk to the bathroom . . .
and I appreciate that I have a bathroom to walk
to. I appreciate that I can dress and undress
myself . . . I appreciate my body's flexibility. I
appreciate that my bodily processes are fine-
tuned and working well. I appreciate toilet
paper . . . I appreciate that I can wipe myself. I
appreciate that I have a flushing toilet. I appreciate the relief I feel . . . I appreciate my ease
with my process . . . I appreciate my amazing,
abundantly healthy and responsive body.

This may not be the sexiest of examples, but that's
kind of the point. Seriously, try doing this exercise the
next time you use the bathroom, or adapt it to any activity.
(NOTE: Every time I read or say the example above, I am
filled with even more things to appreciate about going to
the bathroom! The outline above only begins to cover all
the opportunities for appreciation—that's how it works.)
In fact, the power of appreciation is in its simplicity:
anyone can do it at *any* time. Once you get started, you
will notice that you begin to build momentum in the
exercise. In reading or saying out loud the above example, you will begin to feel your creation energy building.
It is really quite remarkable.

Now, use this same step-by-step, motion-by-motion
appreciation technique in another routine activity, such
as driving a car (you can express gratitude for having

good vision, reactionary ability, knowledge of the roads and rules, pleasing scenery, time to listen to a podcast while in traffic, hearing music you enjoy, a heated seat, etc.). You'll find that this process is easy for the things, feelings, and experiences you love, but the more you do this for the simple, mundane or "auto pilot" activities of life, the more you begin to experience your power as a Creator. This is because you start experiencing the amazing collaborative nature of life and the world around you. The more you focus on and offer appreciation for ALL OF IT—moment by moment—as you are able, the higher the vibration you are creating. And as you begin to focus, resonate, and align to Love instead of fear, the lower vibrations of lack, worry, fear, anger, anxiety, and the like simply stop being distractions because your focus and vibration are not directed there. (Take a quick moment to reread that last sentence and fully take in that the lower vibrations dissipate because *your focus and vibration are not directed there.*) And, when that's the case, you realize how powerful you truly are in controlling the dominant feelings with which your body vibrates.

The bottom line is that what we choose to focus on is a choice—and each of those choices affect our physiology. In situations of true threat, our bodies automatically make us superhuman—with no input of fear—to protect us, followed by the instinctual response of fight, flight, or freeze to get us to perceived "safety." But during the rest of daily life, we choose to put attention on a multitude of thoughts, either fear-based or love-based. The fear-based ones create heaviness, constriction, and even cause dis-ease; the love-based ones create lightness, expansion, creativity, appreciation, and enthusiasm.

Which types will you choose to put your attention on going forward?

CHAPTER SEVEN

The Illusion of Separation

In the Introduction, I shared how my life had become like a storm brewing inside me. One of the worst parts of that storm was how incredibly alone I felt. At the time, I didn't understand that I was never separate from God/Source, so in a way I felt a sense of abandonment, which fueled a sense of fear of not being good enough. Why? Because the core belief that we are separate from God stimulates feelings of unworthiness, as in "If I am separate, it must be because I am not worthy of God's love or attention."

Unfortunately, this belief in separation, and the resulting experience of unworthiness, is translated literally in the mind. What this means is that as you move through your life, your subconscious is scanning your environment and filtering your experiences through your senses and energy, finding evidence of your separation and unworthiness because that is its job—keeping you safe and alive based on what you "tell" it through your thoughts and beliefs. In other words, this fear-driven belief is continually reinforced throughout your physical experience, and from that, you encounter situation after situation that supports your entrenched belief, i.e., "I'm not worthy." Take a moment to reread this paragraph and absorb that. *Your belief, whether true or imagined, is like a magnet that draws experiences into your life that support that belief.*

If you look closely at your life, you will likely discover evidence of this that you probably hadn't realized before. For example, if you grew up believing you weren't smart in some arena, you probably "found" evidence of that throughout your life, which then reinforced your belief, such as being a poor conversationalist or not being good with numbers. Further, when we are rooted in current events, mainstream media, etc., we take in constant stimulation of the idea of separation and unworthiness. This idea can be seen in everything from toothpaste ads to whatever is currently in vogue, from causing cancer to making you fat. The key here is understanding that the mind does not differentiate between real and imagined; it simply responds to what you respond to. Here's an example.

You are watching TV and a commercial plays with the message that if you have this certain product you will be more alive, more powerful, faster, stronger, healthier, sexier, BETTER. While the message may appear innocuous to your conscious mind, every time you see this commercial it stimulates in you, the viewer, a sense that you are not enough without the product. When watching a one-hour program, you will typically see a particular commercial a minimum of four times, and because we tend to be passive watchers—meaning we are there to be entertained and to relax—our filters are down, putting us into pure receiving mode. So with each successive viewing of that commercial, your subconscious becomes stimulated with this message of separation and "not good enough." While you may not be immediately aware of it, your subconscious is processing that data, imprinting the message over and over again.

The consequences of this subliminal messaging are many and actually quite far reaching. Think about this: Have you ever found yourself relaxed while watching TV with your significant other, where things seem fine and then suddenly and without warning, the two of you are bickering about virtually nothing? One of you says something, and that something is interpreted through the stimulated energy of separation and unworthiness in your subconscious, which means your system is on heightened alert. When these seemingly innocuous words enter into the shared space, they are interpreted through this negatively activated filter and perceived as a threat. And what happens when we are threatened, whether real or imagined?

Typically, we react as though our safety is threatened. The result is that the threatened partner returns the attack against the perceived source of aggression: the other person. But here's the real issue. The perception of attack is *incorrect* because the reaction is actually *not* to your partner, but to the stimulation you have been receiving through the TV. Although our minds do not perceive threat from inanimate objects, the reaction comes because the subconscious has mistakenly determined the "cause" of the threat as the words or energy it perceived. So an argument, fight, squabble, or heated exchange of words occurs, stimulating even more agitation. This raises the tension and anxiety, which in turn stimulate this idea of separation and unworthiness even further. It sounds crazy when it's spelled out this way, but the truth is that this belief of separation creates deep-seated emotions that support and encourage feelings of not being safe, understood, or appreciated. These feelings lead to questioning oneself, frustration at not being able to control oneself, and generally bad feelings all around, when all you wanted to do was watch TV and relax!

With all of this tension in the air, your subconscious energy is activated—and feelings of fear grow inside. Sometimes they are manageable, but oftentimes they're not. In the case of the example above, regardless of whether or not there was a resolution, there are lingering feelings that are probably all negative. And what is the primary feeling stimulated? You guessed it: fear. Why fear?

Fear is the undercurrent of all negative feelings—fear of loss, fear of being out of control, fear of separation, fear of not being good enough, fear of not feeling safe. Depending on the situation, you may feel some or all of these, but it is guaranteed that these feelings of unworthiness in some capacity are there if you are willing to look. Unfortunately, this is only the beginning of the chain of events.

Let's return to the argument example and say that you and your significant other reach some level of resolve to the situation. The night winds down and you go to bed, but in the back of your mind you are thinking about what happened, what you said, and what was said to you, replaying and re-envisioning the experience. As you get sleepy, your mind goes to your checklist for the next day at work. You remember a situation that occurred at work that day and know that it needs to be taken care of in the morning. And while a vague sense of uneasiness persists, you drift off to sleep.

The next day, you wake up feeling okay initially. But as you get ready for the day ahead, you are reminded of last night's fight, and a mixture of feelings rise up—anger, sadness, regret, hurt. You have a lot on your plate today, though, so you shift to thinking about the issue at work that needs your attention. Oddly, you start feeling a little uneasy. You cannot seem to settle on any definitive resolution and continue turning it over and over, feeling a little frustrated because you know this situation isn't that big of a deal, yet it feels like it is. After some time passes, however, you are able to calm down and decide on the steps to take.

Upon arriving at work, you are caught off guard with a new and unexpected problem. The shock to the system of this sudden issue stimulates insecurity, and your subconscious is back at work, looking for the threat. Your irritation level increases. You might even get a little short with coworkers or employees. In your mind you are questioning, trying to understand why there is another problem, why things feel out of control, and even possibly feeling overwhelmed by the new problem. It is here that the remnants of fear of unworthiness (still being stimulated by the previous night's events) creep into the mix, and the merry-go-round is in full swing.

Are you able to connect the dots laid out in this example? Every single event and feeling was sourced by the feelings of fear of separation and unworthiness stimulated by the repetitive message from one or more TV commercials. And while I know it seems hard to believe, I encourage you to think about a circumstance where this might have been the trajectory for you. It may not have unfolded exactly as described here, but what's important is that you recognize how each of us is stimulated almost continually with messages of separation, unworthiness, and not enough when we allow ourselves to be completely engaged in mass media and the like. This is not meant to demonize these mediums but rather to bring awareness, as it is only with awareness that you can become conscious of how these messages affect you and how you can better respond to them. In short, to avoid being ruled by fear, you must disengage from the things that promote it in you—and the best way to do that is by heightening your consciousness.

One of the key reasons releasing fear seems so challenging is because fear itself evolves—and it does so by adapting. In other words, the more entrenched someone is in the media and mainstream or mass consciousness, the more adaptable this fear becomes. From the examples provided, you can see that fear moves freely from one area of your life to another, evolving and adapting, influencing just about everything. This is not because of some alien presence, demonic spirit, karma, or God's punishment. *It comes from the core belief that you are separate from God/Source.* And when we hold this belief in separation, it creates the illusion that we are not safe in the world and that there are threats at every turn.

As we briefly touched on in Chapter Three (and will focus on exclusively in Chapter Twelve), your Emotional Guidance System informs you of where you are in relation to your alignment with Self/God/Source. Put simply, negative feelings are the clearest indication that you and your Source are not seeing things from the same perspective—and that you are therefore out of alignment with that larger perspective. It's crucial to note here that *fear of separation and feelings of unworthiness are about as far out of alignment as you can get in this physical experience.* And when that is your reality, fear continues to evolve.

The good news is that while these negative feelings stimulate unpleasant states of being, they are also the indicator of our level of alignment. Remember the exercise we did in the previous chapter about expressing appreciation in a moment-by-moment stream for a mundane activity? The point of that was to show you how to raise your vibration consciously. The same applies here. We have power when we recognize that fear, while it cannot be destroyed, can be released when we elevate our vibration to something greater. Not only does raising your vibration bring you better feelings overall, but it also gives you the ability to see this debilitating illusion of separation. And once the illusion is revealed for what it truly is, you are in the ideal place for quantum, positive transformation to occur.

CHAPTER EIGHT

The "F" Word

I n order to fully grasp the illusion of fear, it is necessary to explore a concept/idea/belief that has created tremendous amounts of terror in people from all walks of life, across all ages, and in nearly every nook and cranny in our culture. This concept/idea/belief is labeled as a word to describe something that most prefer to avoid, and even more strive to never experience. Some people say "It is inevitable, so embrace it," while others claim it is best to reach for "it" fast, early, and often. Many even declare that it and it alone will drive your success. Strangely enough, though, the very definition of this "F" word implies not being enough, doing enough, or having enough.

You can probably guess what this "F" word is. Drum roll, please . . . it's FAILURE. And it is intentionally in all caps because I want you to take a moment and experience what happens when you read the word. In fact, focus on it for ten seconds and watch what begins to happen in your mind and with your emotions. Notice your energy. Now observe how your thought process almost immediately engages the survival instinct. Your heart may begin to beat a little faster, the adrenaline may begin to flow, and a litany of negative thoughts may be triggered, stimulating shame and embarrassment, and even lowering your value as a person, parent, friend, lover, boss, worker, etc.

Ultimately, unless you've been conditioned otherwise, your response to the thought of failure will fall into one of three areas (which are, interestingly, all "F" words as well): fight, flight, or freeze. Remember that this reaction is actually to the *illusion* of a threat to your survival— a very powerful illusion! Think about that for a moment. There is so much collective negative energy and power given to this concept/idea/belief that we believe experiencing failure of any kind is an actual and viable threat to our very survival.

Why? Because we are trained to detest the notion of failure from our earliest years and, as described above, the judgment we carry about it can have a huge impact on us. Simply thinking of oneself as a failure causes a sinking feeling in our psyche. How many people have taken their own lives as a result of believing they've failed?

Once again, we have a concept that stirs within us the most primal emotional experience of separation— and it's no surprise. In many religions, this notion is at the core of their doctrine; the very experience of being human carries the weight of existing as a failed being seeking redemption, hoping for God's grace and favor, or desperate to be saved. If we do not accomplish this redemption or favor, we fail and consequently face the most terrifying, unimaginable pain.

How is that natural?

The answer is, it's not.

This concept/belief/idea of failure is itself flawed, as it is only because of a belief in our separation from Source that the concept of failure is even possible. The truth is: there is nothing in the Universe that fails, EVER. We as human beings have merely determined that it does —and that *we* do. Does that not seem a little strange to you? We are surrounded by endless beauty and perfection, yet when we completely align with our human existence, we arrogantly assume not only that we can fail, but that we are failures from our very origins.

Think about it: as children we explore anything and everything. Our curiosity is boundless and endless. We want to experience, thrive, live, and engage. Left to our own devices, we try lots of things and discard lots of things. We live the adventure of life as it is meant to be lived, through experience after experience. It is only after we are introduced to failure that we begin to pull back from engaging—and, not so coincidentally, it is at this point when our imagination and exploration begin to diminish.

While the time frame is different for everyone, as the evolution depends on your culture, your family, your school, and your religion, this message of failure comes at us in a multitude of ways. For example, think about when you were a little kid watching or being around sports. You were bombarded with the intensity of winning and losing; undeniably clear language and energy was likely used to define those who win and those who lose. As a child internalizes these notions of failure and success, they become impact events in their consciousness that then become belief systems they build their entire life experience around. When a child observes a parent's reaction and emotional response to the success or failure of their favorite sports figure or sports team, for example, the child adopts that perspective, and *more importantly applies that belief to all instances of winning and losing in their experience.* Whether it comes up in taking a test, playing a game, performing in school, or the like, nearly every facet of life becomes structured to support success or failure. Further, the notion of "If I am good, I win; if I am bad, I fail" can take hold, a belief that is surrounded by enormous contradiction. There are many "good" people who apparently fail, and many "bad" people who are apparently successful, yet we will continue to justify the contradiction. This alone tells us that there is something faulty in the concept/idea/belief of failure itself.

Let's look at another example that may confuse this idea of failure: competition.

Whenever we choose to engage in any area of competition, there is a deep desire to prove one's worthiness—a need to beat *my* perceived opponent so I can prove *my* worth, and be a success, by making *you* fail. Of course we cannot compete against another human being to prove worthiness. We can only prove dominance that way.

Ultimately, what we are doing is striving to be the best versions of ourselves. In other words, we can only strive to be, perform, or operate at our highest capacity, and hope that when compared to another person's ability in that same area, we performed at a higher level. However, the standard determination in competition is if you don't win, you failed to measure up or outperform the competition. But this belief is flawed.

A great deal of preparation goes into a competition, whether it's a team sport, an academic tournament, or an individual display of artistic or intellectual prowess or physical talent. Each individual strives to expand their own ability and potential to achieve a greater level of performance (the Olympic games are an excellent example), and to hopefully rise above all the others on the field, in the arena, or in the classroom. But it's not only talent that determines the outcome; all of one's beliefs, ideas, and concepts greatly influence the ultimate performance as well. When we observe someone who competes at a high level, we see that there is usually deep clarity about their experience, and a space/state they "live" in as they prepare—a state many call "The Zone." These people are able to recognize where they are aligned and where they are not aligned within themselves. What this means is, if they do not "beat" the competition, they can reflect on the experience and identify what wasn't completely aligned within themselves. As a result, they will likely strive to work on that specific area of misalignment in order to perform better the next time —and "better" here means exceeding one's own performance.

Let's look at this process more closely.

Within the enhanced or expanded state a person creates, there is a focus on reaching or exceeding specific results, which may indeed be driven by another individual's achievement. However, the person knows they have to find the path to meeting or exceeding those results within *themselves*. For those who achieve this powerful state, they operate in the spectrum of accomplished vs. not, then discern what they can specifically do to improve their performance. Yes, a success/failure model is still present in the greater arena, yet for the more enlightened person, there is deep clarity and understanding that the success/failure model is depleting and puts much of their power, and their ability to achieve the results they desire, outside of Self.

This is why focusing on defeating the other person rarely, if ever, works, because it is self/ego-focused. The truth is, we can only be better than our last performance. We can strive to perform like someone else, but the ability to do so must be found in Self (more on self vs. Self shortly). And when that occurs, the satisfaction and joy of "winning" is found in achieving and aligning with our own highest potential, and then realizing that potential.

But too many people are raised to believe that not

"winning" is not good enough, or even not acceptable. And so they tend to operate in a fear-based fashion—"If I don't win, or be the top performer, I'll *fail*, or I'll be a *failure*." After all, those who don't "win" don't receive the trophies, the medals, the accolades, right?

This is precisely why it's crucial to bring awareness to how these misguided, untrue perceptions—often engrained in us by well-meaning but equally misguided role models—are, like the notion of failure itself, nothing more than illusions. By becoming aware, you gain the conscious ability to reject these erroneous beliefs that drive much, if not most, of our behavior and decisions.

I have already called out that most of us build a foundation upon the concept/idea/belief that we are flawed, unworthy, and separate from God, and that our life is about constantly needing to prove and reprove our worthiness so that in the end we will be judged a success (or failure) by God. But even that's not enough to satisfy the ego/self. We still have a tendency to go over the edge with this concept/idea/belief. We do this by homogenizing our experiences, blending away even our slightest differences in order to build a construct that helps us "discover" our worthiness. Our Tribe. Why? Because we tend to feel most comfortable when the people around us are more alike than different. This "white-washing" is done in religions, schools, and jobs, adding yet another layer to this seemingly complex equation: if we stray from the pre-constructed, socially acceptable homogenized experience, we feel even greater separation, because now not only are we separated from God, but we are separated from our tribe. According to most social models in early times, humans could not survive without support from the group, hence exile or separation from the tribe meant certain death.

Let me be clear: It is crucial that each individual person understand both the inner (God/Source) and outer (tribe) concept and illusion of separation within the context of their own life experience—and this is why.

There are countless souls who cannot abide these layers of supposed separation, so they conform. This can be demonstrated in a multitude of ways: remaining in a religion that doesn't feed their soul; following trends and patterns of others that aren't authentic for them but feel "expected," such as going to college or to a specific institution, finding a "respectable" steady job, drinking socially because friends are, getting tattoos because peers do, etc.; working in the family business; and more.

Others take the opposite route and rebel by forging their own path—leaving the family religion, refusing to follow in their parents' footsteps or fulfill parental desires in their careers, moving away, pursuing their art or passion, living "off the grid," etc., as a way to "find" their worthiness. Those who *conform* may maintain the tribe element of perceived belonging but sacrifice their inner connection with God/Source. Those who *rebel* may miss the feeling of belonging they once had, or they may find a new tribe, but either way are honoring their inner God spark. *What's critical here is that you don't interpret these options as either/or.* As with most concepts and experiences in this life, almost all of us fall on the spectrum from conforming to rebelling.

What we often see in our broader society is that some people are able to break through the outer layers of the belief in separation when it comes to dealing with the "tribe" element, but stumble when they reach the core belief of separation. In simpler terms, their belief expands to feel love and acceptance from outside Self, but they still have not internalized that experience yet. These are the people who tend to return to the fold, unable to sustain life without the tribe because they fail to see or understand the deeper, *internal* belief and feeling of separation from God/Source/Universe that actually drives their experience. The desire for connection, and the lack of understanding of what that connection really is, and to whom, expands feelings of unworthiness, and so they choose to reconnect with the tribe, thinking it will assuage their desire for connection. In short, the powerful pull of this belief in unworthiness and separation (from themselves and important people around them) is simply too strong.

Conversely, there are those who are unwilling to align with these injurious beliefs, and through doing their work (daily practice, meditation, etc.), and through having trust and faith, they are able to find their way to the clarity that is most desired: that of worthiness and oneness. Make no mistake, however, that extricating oneself from this socially entrenched belief structure in separation and fear is challenging. That is because of our innate human desire to belong. In order for a person to have the strength to blaze a trail of faith and trust in Self, he must have the fortitude to separate from the mass consciousness and those who support it, so that he can find clarity within himself.

The good news is that it is absolutely possible to achieve an *inner* sense of connection with God/Source that supersedes any feeling of disconnection a person may experience within the collective, while still feeling an *outer* sense of belonging. How?

Built within every one of us is the desire to know Self. This Self, though, is not the self that we tend to portray. The (capital S) Self is our spark, our God-ness. The other self (lower case s) is our human-ness, our ego.

The distinction between Self and self is necessary in order to see the duality of our experience, and to recognize why there is this distinction. It is also critical in the understanding of the concept of failure.

The belief in separation and unworthiness is developed and nurtured from self to self, meaning that the concepts/ideas/beliefs are developed completely by the ego and transmitted through the culture, as well as generationally. The fundamental idea is that I am unworthy, therefore you are unworthy—and because I feel separate and unworthy, I want my tribe to be in alignment with me. And so it grows, on and on, self to self to self. Then, one day, a single person awakens to the Self. They have an experience of something more, something bigger. It is so compelling that they are initially willing to "suspend" the propagated ideas of self in order to explore this newly experienced Self more fully.

Initially, these new feelings and experiences, as attention is turned to Self, are incredibly powerful. They are exciting feelings of wholeness, wellness, worthiness, and alignment, all of which can be overwhelming to a being who has only experienced the world through self. Yet, through these new feelings, the desire to experience this power of Self more completely and consistently is born. And so the journey of consciousness begins in earnest.

My experience with this came the week I was diagnosed with cancer. I remember sitting in my car, in the parking lot of the doctor's office, having just been informed that I had anal cancer. A weird whirlwind of doctors, nurses, and clinical people scheduling appointments, signing documents, giving advice, setting treatment schedules, and getting me "on board" with their process had just ensued. I distinctly remember the feeling as I sat there: overwhelmed. With tears running down my face, I kept saying the word *cancer* over and over again. And then, a revelation began to occur.

I was already a student of creating my own reality. So, as I sat in my car, I was looking for some surrender and acceptance. I knew I had to step into this new reality differently than I had been operating to that point. As I cried and breathed and contemplated, I began to "see" my own evolution up to that point. I was seeing the energies that my once powerful and uplifting marriage had devolved to, and I became acutely aware of the unhealthy and negative space we had been creating for ourselves for quite a few years. I could literally see the choices and beliefs that brought me to that moment in my car, crying, diagnosed with cancer.

Over the course of the next few days, incredible things began to happen—precisely because I did not resist ANY of the stream of information and clarity that was unfolding inside of me. Every day I would wake up with new clarity of the steps I needed to take to transform the energies I had previously allowed to steer my life. Because I had already manifested physical disease, I realized I would have to approach this with more awareness, openness, faith, and trust than I ever had before. So, I surrendered over and over again to that greater part of myself—my Self. I sought each day to continue to move the needle of my clarity and understanding, and I can tell you that nothing I saw or discovered about myself was horrible, bad, wrong, or broken. I consciously chose NOT to label myself either a cancer victim or cancer survivor, but to focus on *my* energy and beliefs and the things I used to create my current experience. Because I did not identify with or "tribe up," I gave myself absolute permission to just *be* with my process.

Using each day as an opportunity to learn, surrender, appreciate, and grow, I encountered many that were challenging physically, emotionally, mentally, and spiritually. Yet at no time did I attempt to align with the consciousness of cancer. I did not join groups, identify as a cancer patient, or envision a battle to take up. I did not assume competition with the disease process, nor—perhaps most importantly in relation to the theme of this chapter—did I internalize thoughts of failure, or of success for that matter. Instead, I simply welcomed the next step, and then the next step, and then the next step. I began to realize that by taking complete responsibility for this creation in my life, and keeping my focus on my health and wellness, I was undergoing spiritual transformation unlike anything I had ever experienced. I had to evolve my understanding of these two cornerstones, faith and trust, out of their religious association to a spiritual association.

I found the first steps of this transformational journey to be about true faith and trust—what occurs when one's focus is directed toward Self, rather than self. I admit, this is not always easy; we can stay in this split experience for a long time—actively seeking alignment with Self while continuing to operate our lives in self. This is exactly the path of our evolution!

Every day we seek ways to align with Self while releasing the restrictions and beliefs created by the self. So we journey, sifting and sorting, clarifying, learning, and experiencing, all the while searching to achieve our worthiness and connection. As we align more and more with Self, we begin to see that when we act from self, we live in contradiction to our Self. To give you an idea of what this means, think about your unconscious knee-jerk reactions within certain situations, your tendency toward emotions like anger or frustration, your desire to be "right" to protect your ego, your judgmental attitudes toward others, and the like. None of these responses come from Self, but rather from self. What's great is that each step of this journey helps us to identify these contradictions and gives us the opportunity to choose differently. And even better? There is no goal line, no end game, and we will never get it all done when it comes to discovering clarity of Self. It is an evolution, an expansion, and an incredible journey.

Now that you have a deeper understanding of what drives the self, and how actively building and nurturing our relationship with Self awakens us to the illusion of our separation and unworthiness, you can see that as Self, there is no such thing as *failure*—there is only *experience*. Think about it: we are here in this physical world to experience life, and it is impossible to fail an experience. Let me say that again. *It is impossible to fail an experience.* We judge our experience and abilities under the *perception* of success or failure *only* when we are aligned with self/ego. On the flip side, when we are in Self, we recognize that all of our experiences are created *by* us in order to "see" how and where we are attached to the very illusions and beliefs that keep us in separation and unworthiness. In other words, every single experience is a stepping stone to clarity, to our awakening, and to the transformation of our life. This transformation finally occurs when we can completely release our attachment to self and fully align with Self.

Do you now see how life is not about success and

failure? When we are stuck and unable to allow ourselves to experience the Self, it is not failure; it is simply an experience in *contrast*, meaning our awareness of what we *don't* want. This is precisely the basis of free will and the proof that we are creating our own reality. You have full choice to determine whatever experiences you desire. Every experience, and the decision that comes forth from it, becomes part of the next created experience. When there is contrast (something unwanted) and you determine you don't want to repeat that particular manifestation of contrast, you make decisions toward creating better outcomes for yourself. This process is called *evolution*. Each experience not only contributes to your clarity, but it will eventually bring you closer to Self. *It is only the attachment to self that has us believing otherwise.*

And so, when we fear failure, we are telling ourselves this: I believe in my separation and unworthiness, and I will not be able to align with my highest potential, therefore I will be completely separate and unworthy.

I would suggest another "F" word to change that concept: f&%k that!

CHAPTER NINE

Our Subjection to Manipulation

I n this final chapter of Part II, I want to acknowledge that despite everything we've discussed thus far, some people will still fight to keep believing that fear is absolutely not a choice, and that instead, it is a core part of who we are. In response to that, here is the story of a recent experience I had while observing fear manipulation in action. I strongly encourage you to do the same so that you can personally observe the phenomenon.

You may be familiar with the trend of posting prank videos on Facebook and YouTube. A particular genre of these videos focuses on horror, using a demented, evil clown, or a murderous Chucky doll come to life. As people are walking in the park, or heading into a parking garage, or waiting for a bus, the horror character suddenly appears as if in the act of killing someone, or as though they are pursuing the unwitting "victims" of the prank. As you might imagine, these scenarios create strong reactions both for the prank victims and for the viewer. I confess, I have watched these videos numerous times because of my fascination with people's powerful response.

The most fascinating part, however, is that as I observed these videos, I noticed something pretty remarkable. In each situation, there was a gap in every single person's response—despite the flow of action being similar across all pranks. One person, or multiple people, would enter the scene constructed by the prankster, which was being recorded by a hidden video camera, and in every case there was a clear and definitive moment of awareness, immediately followed by a pause, typically very brief, but a pause nonetheless. In this flow from awareness to fear, I would witness a transition moment, one that connected the assessment of the situation to fear. In other words, I observed the transition from awareness, *to something else*, and then to fear. It is the "something else" that is so powerful.

Let's look at it more closely.

In the awareness phase, there is a moment when the subconscious mind engages the five senses to determine the events unfolding. There is also an energetic assessment as the brain attempts to understand what is taking place. The brain registers something familiar, which just so happens to be an object or objects typically associated with fear, e.g., evil clowns, Chucky, or a weapon of some kind. It is important to note here that in every scenario, the people being pranked are at some distance from the action—either several feet to a couple of yards away, and never within immediate striking distance. The pranksters typically run toward and after the "victims," and there is never actually any contact made. I include these details to further emphasize the point that you can, with your own eyes, watch each person take in the scene with no *reaction*, only *awareness*. Because there is no physical harm intended in the prank, there is no immediate sense (energy) of danger, so the energetic assessment does not register a threat to survival. Instead, the five senses survey the scene, looking for elements (memories, pictures) that will bring meaning to the event in front of them, and then the mind instantly makes up a story based on what it finds in the viewer's subconscious experiences. It is *only* at this point that a reaction occurs.

The reaction in these cases could be likened to what is called a *delayed fear response*. This happens when content and meaning are missing from the information available to the brain and must be supplied to fill in the gap of a missing "threat to survival" energy. In short, your mind *imagines* the connection that should terrify you, which you believe and then react to with fear because you are "supposed" to be afraid, according to what your mind has presented.

Why is this so important? Because fear has become such a debilitating energy in the human experience that it sometimes requires acute observation to see it in action. It is precisely in these prank videos that we are able to do this. But even if you prefer not to watch the videos, you are now aware that in order to break down the belief system about fear in ourselves, we must begin looking at how it shows up, when it shows up, and why it shows up. We must become conscious of what is in charge of our consciousness, and how easy it is to manipulate it.

This process of the mind making up circumstances actually happens every day, multiple times a day. Let's look at an example.

How often do you hear someone declare their fear? They might say something like, "I don't like to walk home at night because it's dangerous," or "If I don't pay my taxes on time, the IRS will haul me off to prison." These seemingly innocuous statements, and statements like them, are used all the time by people from every walk of life. They are declarative fear statements generated from a belief about a particular topic. The most paradoxical thing about these statements, and their belief in them, is there is usually next to nothing in their direct personal experience to support the fear. To clarify: *hearing stories about something does not constitute direct knowledge or experience.* I've talked to dozens of people, friends and clients alike, during the writing of this book, and I've asked if they have ever been assaulted, attacked, or threatened during a walk home. Ninety-nine percent of the time, the answer is no. The same is true when I've asked if they personally know of someone who has been assaulted, attacked, or threatened at any time, day or night, when walking home. Ditto for the statement about the IRS.

So what does this show us? That we create belief systems out of anything and everything, even if the situations have never come close to touching our own lives or those we love. Why? Because when we continually subject ourselves to fear manipulation through news programs, the media, and Hollywood, we open up our psyches for programming. Somewhere along the way, you observed on a TV show, in a movie, in a magazine, or in a book, someone who experienced what you are claiming *you* are afraid of. That observation then created an emotional response in you. Typically, this response is empathetic because you feel for the victim; you listen to their story and begin to live their scenario through your own imagination. While there is certainly nothing wrong with empathy, from a scientific perspective, the mind does not differentiate between real and imagined—to the mind it is all the same. So when you create a story in your mind that includes relevant emotions, the story has weight specifically because you are involving *your* mind and emotions.

Once you have fully aligned with the victim's experience and fear, you may as well have experienced it yourself, because now your subconscious has an emotionally charged event that it will store in its warehouse of experiences. The same is true when you watch TV shows and movies that intensely draw you in with adrenaline, especially to the point of fight or flight. This is crucial to understand because your mind will later draw on that "memory" when something shows up in your experience that looks similar. What that means is that your subconscious will match pictures, feelings, or both, with no concern whether the information you provided is real or not. The brain's job is to protect you, ensure your survival, and keep you safe, and it will make up anything necessary to ensure that, based on your emotional responses.

I hope that the dots are beginning to connect for you because once you integrate this powerful understanding, it will change your entire perspective on life. This shift in perspective isn't just good, it's crazy good, and it opens up a world of possibilities and opportunities. Think about it: If you have no knowledge that a person could be jailed for not paying taxes, or if you've never seen or heard of a person being attacked on the street, you can have no fear of that happening. It is only when you witness that these events can occur—whether in real life or through the media—or when someone tells you it's possible, that that potential risk registers in your mind and creates fear. And when our experience is increasingly driven by fear—real or imagined—our subconscious mind consumes enormous amounts of energy to keep the demons at bay, and to help us navigate a continuously narrowing path of choices. If we allow it, our world gets smaller and smaller over time as we begin to limit choices and opportunities. This is because this engrained belief of fear stimulates contraction. As a result, our world must become ever smaller and tightly bordered so we can remain what we inaccurately perceive as safe and alive.

In his inaugural address, Franklin Delano Roosevelt, said, "The only thing we have to fear is fear itself." This declaration was one of the greatest truths ever spoken:

aligning with fear has no upside whatsoever; it only generates more fear. And even then, *it is still a choice*. Being consciously unconscious does not change that.

The more we can look fear in the face and see what it is truly made of, the more we strengthen our clarity and begin to disassemble these limiting beliefs stored in our subconscious. When we realize how easily so many beliefs were put there by events we've never actually experienced, it is truly mind-blowing. (Remember, beliefs are simply created by repetitive thought, both individually and collectively.) Yes, all of these fear-based events *can* happen, but unless we live particularly reckless (substitute *unconscious*) lives, the likelihood is really quite slim.

And so, now that we've unveiled some of the most engrained and accepted roles fear plays, and you have realized you have more power over fear than you ever knew before, let's dive into Part III, where we will explore ways you can take your newfound empowerment and make choices toward being liberated from the vast majority of fear that tends to hold you back from living the life you were meant to live.

PART III

LIVING IN
LIBERATION
FROM FEAR

CHAPTER TEN

What Does Transformation Really Mean?

I have used the term "transformation" multiple times throughout this book, and now it's time to fully explore what it means for YOU in relation to living in liberation from fear.

First, let me be clear about what I mean when I use the word transformation. I define it as transcending; or going beyond the limits of what you have previously believed, thought, or felt about or toward any circumstance or experience, while still including "what was, what is, and what will be." Meaning, when we transform ANYTHING, we expand well beyond our limits, *and* we include all that came before. Here's why.

Transforming is a resistance-free state. This is important because in transforming, we truly recognize that everything we have experienced is an integral—and necessary—part of who we are. So, to be clear: To *transcend* is to go beyond the limits of one's beliefs, ideas, or thoughts, and to *include* is pure acceptance of all that came before. For example, you don't become someone different, as in starting off as Jim and ending up as Paul. Instead, you start off as unconscious, disempowered little Jim and become clear, powerful, engaged, and authentic Super Jim. This is what I mean when I say you transcend *and* include what you have learned from all aspects of your being as you step into your transformation. The process opens you up to more of who you truly are—your Authentic Self.

This process of personal transformation is by no means random. It does not happen by accident; in fact, there is a science to transformation. However, you may be currently operating from a place or state of consciousness that does not allow you to see that clearly—yet. You may think of transformation as a spiritual journey, and it is. But what you may not realize is that you are already living that journey right now.

We have all come into this physical life to experience transformation, or rather, to experience our evolution in action. While the events and circumstances of our lives may appear haphazard, coincidental, accidental, random, or without logic or continuity, that is truly an illusion on the grandest scale—one that is built on a particular foundation, and that foundation is fear.

Prior to engaging this life, as part of your soul's journey of transformation and evolution, you had a clear plan, or better yet, *desire*. You set up the circumstances of this life you were about to enter, ensuring yourself the greatest opportunities for success. Where it all started to go (apparently) sideways is when you arrived in this amazing playground of time and space called physical reality.

It may help you to think of your coming into this life as if you were starting a new job. You know that feeling, right? You're likely excited, nervous, and anticipatory, while at the same time feeling ready, equipped, and skilled. Maybe you've even worked for years to prepare for this new position. Regardless, there is a lot going on— emotionally, mentally, spiritually, and physically.

You come in on your first day, thinking you are prepared, and then overwhelm ensues. You are inundated with scores of new information. You're introduced to a lot of new people as you're shown around your new place. Not only are you trying to find your way around, but you are attempting to get a read on the people you work with, most importantly your new boss, and there is a stream of never-ending questions. Where is the bathroom? How do I do [fill in task]? When is lunch? How should I behave? Should I be reserved? Should I be outgoing? You want to demonstrate that you belong and make a great impression. But these first few days or even weeks might be spent feeling insecure and frustrated that you're not yet completely on top of your new responsibilities. Maybe you come home at the end of the day drained and overwhelmed, unsure if you are "getting" it and struggling to find your rhythm, or even feeling like you've failed or are failing. Does this sound vaguely familiar?

But as we discussed at length in Chapter Eight, failing is something you never *were* doing or *are* doing now; in fact, you never have or will fail because *you cannot fail this experience called life.* In contrast, you were, and maybe still are, *adjusting.* For some people, this adjustment takes a short amount of time; for others it takes decades. Either way, it's ALL good!

Starting a new job and immersing yourself in the unfamiliar is eerily similar to what happened when you were born into this life. You prepared everything you needed to take on this new "job": selecting your parents, your environment, your gender (more on this in Chapter Fourteen)—all of the specific details and energies to serve your desire. You were highly qualified and had amazing experience, but just like in any new "job," you were overwhelmed by your unfamiliar surroundings in the physical world. No matter how many times you had done this before, getting acclimated and adjusted simply took time.

It's the same in your new job. After you've been in your position for a while, you begin to see the "reality" of the experience, which includes some of the negative aspects of your new environment. While these things are merely part of the larger experience, if you want to you can choose to focus on and engage in these negative aspects and become mired in the drama. But what you may not recognize is that the more you *engage* the negative aspects, the more you *see* them and *experience* them, the more you become *focused* upon them, and the more you *create* them. The good news is that the same is true when you focus on the positive aspects, such as what you love about your work, being productive, and creating at your highest level. In sum, the more your focus is on either the positive or the negative *experience*, the more your overall experience will become filled with a positive or negative *perspective*. YOUR LIFE IS NO DIFFERENT.

What also happens with a new job is that as you become more accustomed to and aligned with your new circumstance, you begin to find your rhythm and thrive. You build desires and set goals. You may even start seeing a pathway to something bigger and better. Opportunity shows up all around you. Once again, YOUR LIFE IS NO DIFFERENT.

Today, science is able to study and map our transformational abilities through research in the neuroplasticity of the brain—which explores our ability to change our physiology, our capability of monitoring and shifting our thinking, the changeability of our DNA, quantum physics, and so much more. Why is this important to us? Because all of this discovery reflects that indeed we have the ability to do virtually *anything*. Nothing in the universe, our world, or ourselves is stagnant. Everything on this beautiful planet is evolving, changing, and transforming. Many fear the idea of transformation because of a belief that it means to become someone or something different—and ultimately you do. But the change you experience is from the inside out. It doesn't happen *to* you, it happens *within* and *through* you.

The caterpillar becoming a butterfly is the most

poignant and powerful illustration of transformation that exists in our physical world. The caterpillar devolves from its former self within the cocoon into a literal soup, completely unrecognizable, yet it is not becoming something other than itself; rather, it is becoming the best expression of itself. The changes the caterpillar experiences are instigated and actualized from within itself. In other words, transformation will never change something into another thing that is unrecognizable to itself; transformation is simply the act of always evolving into the best possible version of whatever is transforming. Worm to butterfly, coal to diamond, water to ice, ice to water, human to superhuman. You get the idea. When we transcend all that came before, while including those experiences as part of who we are, it leads us to transform our experiences, consciousness, and thought processes, which in turn changes our world. I say "our" world because transformation changes *your* perspective of the world, and therefore changes your relationship to everything in it.

I realize that these concepts may seem profound and difficult to grasp at first. If that's true for you, just remember that everyone is having their own experience and creating their own perspective all the time, and at the *same* time, in our time and space playground. In short, we are all building our life experience through our perspective of our life and the world.

So how does being liberated from fear play into all of this?

Let's say you have an incredible transformation, yet see that the rest of the world is continuing on in its own perspective, one that appears limited and diminished. Within this worldview, you may be eager to share your new experience, hoping that some people will "get it"— and if you're fortunate, some will. However, many others probably won't. This is where you have to understand that until they find themselves in that space where they, too, are ready to transcend the "what is" of their experience, they simply won't be on the same page as you—and that's okay. The Science of Transformation is all about unraveling the formula that stimulates *your* growth and expansion. Put another way, if others are holding themselves in a fear space—or keeping themselves held away from some level of expansion for reasons of their own—it doesn't have to affect *you*. Their fear doesn't have to be *your* fear. Why? Because ***fear is a choice***. Always. You have the freedom and the power to observe what occurs when we choose fear, and when we do not choose fear. It is your prerogative, as the science exemplifies, to experiment and explore, to draw conclusions and make decisions based on the results, and then implement and live in that new understanding. You get to do this every single day.

What's even more exciting is that the Science of Transformation is about you tapping into your greatest potential, exploring all possibility, experiencing everything you desire, changing and evolving from it, and coming to a deep clarity about it all. And that process never ends. It is not only what you came here to do, but it is in this space that you finally accept and *know* that fear is no longer required in your life journey because all of it is a delicious unfolding. Best of all, when you realize that fear is not a constant or a certainty as you may have been conditioned to believe, transformation into your higher Self becomes inevitable.

CHAPTER ELEVEN

Getting to Know Your Emotional Guidance System

n Chapter Three, I gave you a brief introduction to the concept of our Emotional Guidance System. In this chapter, we're going to do a deep dive into it, because understanding this "system" in the body is one of the surest ways you can experience quantum, positive transformation and liberation from fear.

But before we look more closely at how our Emotional Guidance System works, we must understand that fear is nothing more—and nothing less—than an emotion. It is part of our emotional experience, no different from happiness, sadness, excitement, depression, anger, apathy, satisfaction, etc. In other words, *it has no more weight than any other emotion, despite the fact that we often give it more weight in our consciousness.* So why do we have a tendency to want to demonize fear, go after it, attack it, and destroy it? Because we've been trained to do so. We are told to "confront our fears," "get back on the horse," "have nerves of steel," and other similar idioms as a way of combating this "demon" among us. As a result, we often feel the need to strike out against this thing that is zapping our talent, strength, power, ability, and success. In fact, we have given fear so much of our power that we have incarnated it and given it life, as though it were its own entity.

When we demonize fear, we put massive resistance into an already resistant situation. No one wants to fan the flames of fear, yet that's precisely what scores of people do in putting greater and greater attention on "slaying" it. Instead, I invite you to embrace an entirely different view of fear—and indeed of all our human emotions. And that is within the context of our Emotional Guidance System (EGS).

One of the core tenets of the Law of Attraction is understanding our emotions and their purpose, or rather, where our true alignment is. Put simply, when a question stimulates a negative emotional response, that response is an opportunity to understand how out of alignment you are with the Truth of who you are. What this means is, when you experience negative emotion, you are being informed clearly, and in no uncertain terms, that you and your Higher Self/God/Universe/Source are not seeing or experiencing the situation or circumstance in the same way. In other words, within this out-of-alignment experience, you and your Higher Self are not on the same page.

How often have you been confronted by some task or opportunity that, when you think about it, causes your energy to drop—or "spin" as I like to call it—meaning you begin a downward spiral of emotional and mental chatter. The more you push into it, the worse it feels. So many of us have received the message from various self-help books to just push through our resistance and make it happen! And so, it's no surprise you automatically assume that your inability or unwillingness to complete whatever it is you think you need to complete is because you are either being lazy, afraid, incompetent, or whatever language you typically choose. But regardless of the words, the result is the same: *your energy doesn't feel good, but you persist anyway.*

What I know with certainty is that when you do this, your results will not be what you anticipated or wanted. Even if you are successful by pushing through, you will find that you are battered by interference after interference, delays, missed communication, misunderstandings, the list goes on. You may succeed in completing the task, but the likelihood is that you will not be happy with the results, and, perhaps worse, will find yourself extremely frustrated by the process.

In this situation, what you will recount is not the accomplishment, but instead a rehashing of the drama and frustration you experienced attempting to complete the task. When you are negatively focused this way, you will feel only a mild sense of accomplishment, if any, because of how awful the process was. What is shocking and disconcerting is that we actually think this is "normal," that this is the way life is supposed to be.

But when you understand that your emotions—all of them—are your guidance system, you not only start to pay attention to how you feel, but you realize that your emotions are an incredibly powerful tool!

Let's consider having a task or opportunity before us again, but this time we will allow ourselves to be guided by our emotions.

Say this task causes your energy to drop, creating a negative emotional state. The emotions you feel may be mild irritation, frustration, sadness, anxiety, depression, apathy, or any combination or variation of these.

At the moment you are able to recognize the emotion(s), there is only one thing to do: STOP! I hear you saying, "What?! Stop? I can't do that. I have to act on this. I have to get it done!" But trust me on this. At the moment you recognize that the situation is causing negative emotions in you, I want you to stop, and here is why.

1. Your Emotional Guidance System is telling you that you (self) and your Highest Self do not have the same viewpoint of this situation. In other words, your negative experiences, expressed through self/ego, are two or more disparate energies seeking resolution. These energies are: a) the situation, b) your reaction to it based on your beliefs, and c) The broader perspective of Self/God/The Universe. The negative feeling, and the intensity of it, are showing you, through feeling, how far out of alignment (with Self/God/The Uni-

verse) you are in the moment. This means it's time to step away and assess.

OR

2. You are either not clear yet, don't have enough information about it, don't understand it correctly, or need more clarity regarding some aspect of it that you currently don't have. Therefore, it is time to step away and assess.

It is at this point where you are likely to experience the strongest feelings of resistance, meaning that your mind will be in a "spin cycle," or rather, in a noise-making and flawed logic–making attempt to convince you that if you stop, you are a loser, a failure, a wimp, etc. It is vital to recognize that all of that chatter or noise is merely reaction created out of the mind/ego, which causes a highly charged negative emotional state, but is *not* the current reality.

Don't attempt to push through it. Stop. Breathe. Assess. Recognize that you are not in alignment, and don't try to immediately surpass it because you think it's the [brave, professional, expected, etc.] thing to do.

I recognize this will push a lot of people's buttons. As I said before, we've been trained to hold fast to beliefs like, "I must push through." "I can get this done if I just grin and bear it." "I am an achiever!" "I must be a success, not a failure." Yet this is merely a manifestation of one of humanity's biggest myths: "By use of will, I will achieve."

Make no mistake: when you are in alignment, *effort* may be necessary, but *struggle* is not. There may be no more important takeaway in this chapter than this, so I want to be certain you take this in fully. *Effort* is about creating momentum in your energy toward that which you desire. You can activate this momentum by thought, feeling, and activity. Your effort is inspired by your alignment. On the other hand, *struggle* is resistance that is created when you are not aligned, and in attention to, where your energy and Emotional Guidance System is attempting to guide you. Struggle is using will to push against what is perceived as unwanted or in the way of what you think you want.

So, you may be asking, is every emotion a message from our Higher Self, guiding us toward our most aligned path?

And the answer is YES.

Similar to intuition, or the "God voice" that speaks to you from inside, your Emotional Guidance System is always on. The question is, "Which voice am I paying attention to?"

In all significant events and decisions in your life that have given you some level of unrest or maybe even upended your life in some way, if you honestly examined them, you would recognize that your intuition and your Emotional Guidance System were giving you a signal of misalignment, first by a feeling of your energy dropping.

With intuition, you may say, "Something told me not to do that," or "A little voice warned me about that," or "I had a gut feeling but ignored it." You may even sense a screaming, visceral NO.

With the Emotional Guidance System, you may feel a surge of anything from uneasiness to be being repelled, or emotions such as hurt, anger, depression, anxiety, and the like. It is important to note here that the stronger the emotion, the greater the need for you to gain understanding about your lack of alignment with that broader perspective we spoke of earlier. In either case, it's time to stop and assess! Side note: It is also important to remember that intuition always comes first, but if you are not aligned with that "voice," you will then experience it through your EGS.

Even a minor feeling of unrest deserves your examination. Remember, when this occurs, it is the moment to stop, sense the alignment or lack of it with your Higher Self/Source, gain more clarity, disregard the mind chatter, and then make a decision.

Take the following examples and see if you can apply one or more of them as similar situations come up for you.

I was two years into my podcast, and things seemed to be cooking along nicely. My podcast partner and I had recently established a new vision for our work and the impact we wanted to create. Not long after, however, things began to unravel. The incidents that occurred over the next few weeks created deep upset and unrest inside of me. I found myself dreading doing the podcast, and I would sit in meditation, day after day, seeking clarity and a resolution, while also encouraging myself and making every attempt to shift my energy. This went on for weeks. Although nothing had been resolved as yet, I would talk myself into a better place. Regardless, every time I was about to go on, my energy would bottom out and I'd have to really work to find some alignment for the show. I realized I had to make a big decision, but I also realized I was struggling with my own self-worth, which was influencing this challenging experience too. After three weeks of living this conflict, I came to realize that nothing in the entirety of my experience would change until I stepped into my clarity—and I finally found it during one of my meditations. The "secret" to releasing my energy was Love. I surrendered to it, found clarity in my communication with my cohost, and stepped completely into the necessary change. Once I crossed that threshold, everything started to flow and unfold in spectacular fashion. The concerns I had vanished, and I discovered a new clarity of my worthiness, which lead to an even greater feeling and experience of alignment.

———

Years ago, my editor received an inquiry from a prospective client with whom she felt a strong connection to his book's content, but right away felt unease with the author himself. The red flags were evident from the start, but she ignored them because she believed in the project and sincerely wanted to help this person bring the book to life. However, in ignoring her Emotional Guidance System's signals that the partnership would be out of alignment with her, she ended up spending four of the most stressful, mis-aligned months working with this client. Now, if emotional red flags show up for a prospective partnership, she wastes no time heeding them and politely declines the opportunity as not be-ing the best match.

———

A very dear friend was having serious issues with his marriage. He was unhappy and frustrated, and he wanted to make his spouse wrong about everything regarding their connection and alignment. He had created a grand litany of sto-ries about his experience, built up an arsenal of evidence to support his viewpoint. and decided to have conversation with his spouse about end-ing their marriage. We worked on helping him to step into the situation from a "win-win" perspective, and he agreed not to approach the conversation until he was not in reaction or judgment. That took some time, and he continued to prepare his space until the night of the conversation arrived. When it did, he approached it with clarity and Love. And the conversation he thought he was going to have—about getting a divorce—changed radically because of the work he did. As a result, they had one of the best connected conversations of their marriage, and they mutually agreed to move forward together, but in a much more conscious, open way.

Of course, your Emotional Guidance System is also working for all the positive emotions as well. In these cases, your emotions are like bumper guards on a bowling lane, demonstrating the power of your alignment. That powerful alignment is guiding you toward the things that light up your soul, utilize your gifts, and keep you in alignment with your Higher Self and universal flow. While these tend to be easier to follow (unless, of course, you're afraid to be happy!), it's the signals we receive that let us know we're *out* of alignment with God/ Higher Self that we typically need to learn not to ignore. The thing is, we are likely to be as unconscious of the positive impact of our EGS as we are the negative. But, as you become more conscious and attend to your alignment, you will find that you simply begin to respond to your EGS wherever it is. If you are feeling good, you appreciate more, and you consciously seek more of that good feeling and the things that created it. If you are feeling bad, you also appreciate more, and consciously seek better feeling thoughts as you refocus your energy and vibration back to those things you desire.

And when it comes to fear in particular, it's critical to remember that fear is merely an emotion—and like all emotions, it is part of our Emotional Guidance System. In simple terms, whatever you fear and whenever you fear, you can be sure that your physical self and your Higher Self are not looking at things the same way. Why? Because if your Higher Self/Source Energy were in fear, *your* feelings of fear would be in alignment with it, and there would be no rub or conflict! Let me say that again. If your Higher Self/Source Energy were in fear, *your* feelings of fear would be in alignment with it. But since your Higher Self never fears, whenever *you* experience fear, you are out of alignment with that All-Knowing Source Energy. With that in mind, instead of internalizing the fear and possibly letting it consume you, simply take a deep breath, then say:

"I'm out of alignment right now with God/my Higher Self. I am *making up a story* right now, based on the situation I'm experiencing, to suit my negative emotional response. My Higher Self is having a different experience, and I want to see from that perspective. I'm either projecting fear about something that will likely never hap-

pen, or I'm experiencing a sense of fear because
my Higher Self—which knows everything—is *not*
in fear, and I am clearly out of alignment with
that higher knowing."

You can also repeat the phrase, "I am aware of my
emotions; therefore, I am not my emotions."

Once again, your emotions are not YOU. They are
merely indicators of alignment with Source, and fear is
only one such indicator. Fear is NOT fight or flight; that
response is part of the survival instinct. Fear is an emotion, plain and simple.

I hope you will leave this chapter with the knowledge that you can trust yourself and your Emotional
Guidance System. I guarantee that when you do, things
will begin to flow much more easily in your life. Every
time you honor this system, your clarity will become
stronger, your stress levels will reduce dramatically, and
you will arrive at better, more effective answers, solutions, and abilities, with greater ease and tranquility. As
you release resistance (i.e., negative emotions), you will
easily come into alignment with God/Source. And when
you come into alignment, life becomes about ease and
flow, not struggle.

Even better? ***Once you are in alignment, you are no
longer able to be manipulated by or with fear.***

CHAPTER TWELVE

Turning Thoughts into Things Through Imagination

Have you ever thought about the fact that everything, *everything*, that exists in our material world was once only a thought? That someone experienced a need or desire for something, and then, through imagination, focus, and intention, that person created a "something" in this physical reality? Everything from pop-up books to bongo drums, stuffed animals to pet costumes, ball-point pens to back-up drives, wind-up toys to rocket ships—anything imaginable in the realms of education, entertainment, comfort, humor, utility, technology, fun, exploration, and more have been dreamed up in someone's mind, and are now part of our human existence. And think about this: Had fear held these people back, how many wonderful inventions wouldn't have been realized?

When we take a moment to observe the astonishing outcome of things like merely pressing numbers on a phone (connecting with someone's voice anywhere on the planet), clicking a mouse (making things magically appear and disappear on a computer monitor), or watching a TV show (beaming millions of particles that create moving images with sound onto a screen in your home), we recognize that there is truly no end to the power of what our imaginations can manifest, even when logic seems to defy it—and certainly when fear doesn't hold us hostage.

How does this actually work energetically?

The process of creation begins with the *desire* to create. As desire itself begins to draw to it compatible elements of energy, the desire begins to take on new form: thought. The vibration of the desire then slows down, becoming something tangible to the mind. While these thoughts still exist outside the arena of time and space, it is here that these more specific thoughts enter into the realm of imagination—where we can consciously entertain and explore desire outside the confines of time and space, or rather, play with these desires as energy to manipulate, explore, expand, consider, watch, and even feel our desire become real without actually manifesting it in the physical world. This imagination playground creates a powerful energy field for our desire, and as the vibration of the desire strengthens and builds momentum, the cooperative elements—all energies and circumstances necessary to manifest the desire from non-physical to physical reality—are integrated into this momentum.

Once this impetus is in motion, we play with these

desires within imagination for as long we need to bring them into complete focus and fully realize them outside of time and space. Note that this period of play is a *critical part of creation*, and that when we don't allow fear to disrupt that playtime, the imagination builds not only momentum and intensity, but energetic pathways between the non-physical and the physical. These energy pathways are the very links that the creating human being will use to align their desire (non-physical) with their physical reality.

To understand alignment, let's look at it this way: Your alignment is like an anchor on a boat. The water the boat sits in is in constant motion, even if it appears as though that motion is directionless. In using an anchor to maintain the boat's current position, it stays in the same general area. This idea is very similar for us as humans. We are energy beings, swimming in a sea of constantly moving energy, even when we may feel directionless at times. The way we anchor ourselves is through *alignment*, meaning we choose a place/space to anchor ourselves in this physical reality, which we do based on our understanding of our own energy. If we're largely unconscious, our alignment—and our creations— will be as well.

If we are conscious, we then consciously choose where to anchor, or align, in a way that creates a vibrational harmony between our desire and our physical reality. This then allows for all kinds of serendipity, or "Universal magic," to unfold! This is why it is so important to clearly understand and embrace what alignment is and does for us, because *alignment is critical to creation.*

When we are creating, the object of our creation must be something that aligns with our vibration. In basic terms, it is a process of "like attracts like." In building these energy pathways between the physical and non-physical through active use of the imagination, if the vibration of the desire in the imagination resonates with our human energy field, then this energy of the specific desire begins to become matter. It is as though the desire itself is being pulled or drawn into physical existence through the alignment of the human being's energy with the energy of the desire. Said another way, the aligned human energy field basically acts like a magnet, drawing to it whatever is desired or believed. And therein lies the rub.

While I don't want to enter discouraging territory within a conversation about manifesting desires, it is vital that you know this magnet of attraction will attract what is conscious *and* what is unconscious. That is, your magnet of attraction brings to you whatever is in your energy and activated by your mind, whether you are aware of it or not, and this could include fear.

What can prove difficult for people is coming to the understanding that the point of attraction for many emanates from unconscious beliefs, and even when you are working at conscious creation, the energy of what is below the conscious threshold is a much stronger magnet, specifically because it is infused with the deep emotional content that made it a belief from the very beginning.

For example, if you are working hard toward getting a promotion at work, but in your subconscious mind, you hold old beliefs of your unworthiness and/or counterproductive beliefs about money and your relationship to it, you will likely find that the promotion frustrates you, or actually eludes you. This is not because the effort isn't there; it's because the energetic magnet of your subconscious is attracting to the stronger vibration. In this case, that vibration is that you're not deserving, or aren't good with money. Therefore, the promotion doesn't manifest, or manifest as quickly. Understand here that you can absolutely create anything you desire; *you just have to be clear where you are creating from.*

While how to heal these old belief patterns is beyond the scope of this chapter, I nonetheless want you to have awareness of these powerful, unconscious energies so that if you're struggling to manifest your desires, or the opposite of what you're striving to create is manifesting, you can find the answers and solutions within yourself, not within circumstance.

The next crucial piece of the creation puzzle is this: when we are truly in imagination, we must waste no time trying to figure out *how* our desire will manifest. Instead, we expressly spend our time and energy *seeing* it happening, *feeling* its joyful manifestation, *witnessing* the impact of it in our life, *celebrating* its arrival, and *enjoying* all the wonderful feelings it creates. This is what paves amazing pathways in our physical energy system, and it is here that the process of physical creation begins.

This time spent in imagination cannot be underestimated, as it is here that we determine whether or not this thing we desire is truly what we wish to manifest in our physical reality. As we explore the desire with our imagination, we use our physical senses, along with our energetic capacity. Most importantly, we *feel* into it to ensure it is indeed the item we want to own, the business we want to start, the house we want to live in, the trip we want to take, the car we want to drive, the solution to our problem, etc.

It is important to reiterate here that the process of exploring in the imagination does not include any focus on HOW. When using your imagination, you must see things as done. Don't spend any time trying to figure things out, and definitely don't entertain fear of them not being feasible; simply see the object within your imagination coming to fruition. Questions like, "How will I get rich?" or "How will I plan my next vacation?" are operations of your rational mind. In contrast, you want to see and experience things and events within your imagination as they are occurring. This is a significant understanding to embrace because creation is not predicated on *how* it will manifest; creation is activated when the desire aligns with your vibration. In fact, the creative process is actually shut down by bringing *how* into the equation. Why?

"How" is a function of our rational minds, i.e., our ego. And our attachment to "how" these desires will come about is actually part of the evolution of, you guessed it: fear. You may think that masterminding the *how* is a natural next step. Most people do because we've been conditioned to believe that. But in actuality, when we ask *how*, we disconnect from our creative process, and more importantly, we disconnect from our true Self. How many times have you shot down a dream because you almost instantly feared it could never happen? Whether you doubted your ability, your luck, or your resources, the doubt stemmed from the belief that you were not enough, which is itself a belief that you are separate from creation. It not only reflects a lack of trust in your innate ability to create, but it is in opposition to who you truly are.

You are creation.

You are surrounded by creation.

You live in creation.

Yet many of us think creation is something that occurs outside of us.

But remember that when we stay in imagination and allow the energy to build there, energy pathways develop. These pathways grow and expand based on the beliefs we call Faith and Trust (Faith = complete confidence in Self. Trust = state of being responsible to Self). When we allow ourselves to fully accept and embrace faith and trust, we are able to create with abandon and without limitation and judgment. It is only through these qualities that we allow ourselves to fully experience, in consciousness, the end result we desire to create. Said another way, within the realm of trust and faith, we "see" our desire realized in full detail without attachment or limitations as to *how* that desire will happen. In short, we reside in the realm of infinite possibility.

You are probably beginning to internalize that these two qualities of faith and trust help us to align with God/Universe, because when we are aligned, we can tap into the unlimited potential of all creation. In imagination we do not yield to limitation, and we are therefore able to create anything. This is precisely why we have technology that most humans have no idea how to explain. These "miraculous" devices came to fruition because the inventors were in full alignment with Source energy, and they believed wholeheartedly in their desire for more effective ways to communicate and connect, without knowing *how* that might happen, or what it might look like.

Think about it: when you are immersed in your imagination, you believe you are all powerful. You can see the end result in physical form because your trust and faith are in alignment with God/Universe. It is only when you doubt the possibility of your creation, or get caught up in the "how," or believe you are separate from Source energy, that this vision dissipates. But when you use your imagination without boundaries, you strengthen your connection to all possibilities, accepting and recognizing that the spark (God/Universe) in you can do anything. And when you are in alignment with trust and faith, you honor that spark in you, that God part of you that can create worlds.

Now that you understand the infinite power of

faith and trust, you can see the truly destructive nature of fear. When you allow your vibration to stay aligned with fear rather than with faith and trust, you create inconsistency in your life experience and in the execution of concepts like the *Law of Attraction* and the *Laws of Creation*. This inconsistency is caused by your own inability to imagine deeply and align your energy with your desires.

Once again, this is due to fear-based attachment to *how* your desire is going to manifest.

Look, I get it. Most of us aren't raised to believe that merely having a clear desire, nurtured by our imagination, is enough for it to manifest. We are either conditioned to believe that we are inferior to an all-powerful God, or we're not taught that we are just as much a creator as God/Source. Think about it: when a child is conceived, we don't spend time thinking about *how* we created this child on a microscopic or biological level. We marvel in the miracle of creation, and our trust and faith in that creation allows it to come forth. Science gives us some ideas of the *why*, but ultimately cannot answer the absolute divinity of the *how*. And yet, creation continues.

The final piece in the creation process of bringing the non-physical into physical reality is language. Once we have adopted language, we forever alter our creative process because it is through our words that we express our thoughts and feelings, which in turn become our creations.

The process of learning to speak is a highly powerful

process of translation: energy is translated into thought and then thought into language. Unfortunately, bringing ideas born in the imagination into something more concrete through words can be limiting. This is because as we begin to talk about our dreams, we are no longer simply "being" with them, and we tend to filter these dreams through judgment and assessment, which takes us back to where fear creeps in. Further, when we speak to others about our ideas, we often dilute the energy, and more importantly, we take on outside viewpoints. Are you sensing what typically occurs now? Depending on your chosen audience, a potentially powerful creation can quickly morph into an idea that no longer seems viable, strictly from one or more comments that deem it so. This input alters our creative "being" process in relation to our dream, often allowing fear to creep in, and diminishing our faith and trust in that process.

At some point, we will indeed have to use language to invent that gadget, build that house, buy that car, plan that vacation, etc. But the point here is that we must carefully choose who is in on the dream during the period when we energetically bring those cooperative components together in our mind to make it manifest. Remember, as long as we are in alignment with God/Source, and we continue to use our imagination to conjure the desire into reality, outside influence—or the *how*—is not necessary, and is even often detrimental. If you bring people into your idea while still in its infancy, or even if you've fully imagined it and know it's what you want, their opinions of why or how, or of the likelihood of making it happen, can kill that energy. Words are that powerful. This does not mean that every dream comes to fruition in a vacuum, only that when you bring it forth with language—even when speaking to yourself—you are mindful of the level of nurturing your idea will receive, or not.

We are powerful creators, and imagination is a key ingredient to creating on the physical plain because it is the one way we can consciously access the non-physical realms and build the energy of our desires. As you embark on your next creative journey, remember this:

You are creation realized from the imagination of the Divine. Does it matter *how* that is so, or just that it *is* so?

CHAPTER THIRTEEN

Cultivating the Unique Spark That Is You

Imagine what our human experience would be like if we embraced our Spark, that aspect of each of us that is God. What if instead of moving through a treadmill of human experience with no clarity of purpose, other than to go through the pre-determined stages of childhood, adolescence, young adulthood, adulthood, middle age, etc., we recognized that each individual Spark is here to evolve its own unique expression and understanding of itself? And what if we spent the majority of our time and energy cultivating that unique Spark?

Perhaps the best way to even consider such an inspired endeavor is to understand why most of us *don't* currently spend the bulk of our existence focused on this, which is twofold.

First, we tend to exist detached or separated from the inner core of our being. In other words, we live in a world believing we are separate from that which we are created—

or God/Source. Think about that for a minute. This is akin to, as a parent, believing that your own children are not worthy and are separate from you—and therefore have to strive their entire lives for your love and connection. Can you see the flaw in the logic of this thinking? Would you expect your child to have to *earn* your love, or would you constantly assert their separateness from you, as if you had nothing to do with their creation? Of course not. It is the same with our Divine Creator.

Second, the reality of our Spark is not entertained because science says it is not yet "provable," that they cannot test for it or verify it. What?! Our very existence is the proof! How can we witness the evolution of a logic-defying physical body that performs untold functions on our behalf every second of every day, yet not be willing to embrace the Spark that animates it?

In the last chapter, we talked in depth about the power of creation. I want to revisit that here because as humans, we often willingly and consciously deny the source of our own existence, failing to recognize that our own Spark is what we seek to understand. *We* are the physical manifestation of Creation! Why do we insist on dumbing down this extraordinary reality?

The answer is plain and simple: Fear. Fear that we shouldn't equate ourselves with God as powerful creators, because we've largely been taught that we are inferior, while God is superior and dislikes anyone who dares think otherwise. But as we discussed at length in Chapter Three, this is nothing more than conditioning to keep you small, and to keep those "in power" (e.g., heads of many orga-nized religions) looming large with unmerited authority.

The truth is that we are on the precipice of a tremen-dous leap in consciousness, with each Spark exploring, reaching, learning, seeing, expanding ever forward to that incredible realization that "I am God" (or, if it's more com-fortable for you, "to be in complete one-ness with God, who resides within me"). Each single consciousness has been given the opportunity to explore the furthest reaches of this time and space reality, seeking to understand and know itself fully and completely. Each Spark is meant to unfold in experience, awareness, and clarity.

What's even more extraordinary is that every level of consciousness humans have evolved through is still present on the Earth at this time. From prehistoric con-sciousness that seemed very limited, through all of the recorded consciousness shifts—mythical, rational, scien-tific, industrial, technical, transrational (going beyond or surpassing human reason). All of these levels of con-sciousness are still active on the planet right now! What's more, each one is able to interact and explore with the other. I know this is a mind-bending concept, so let's keep it simple by looking at it this way: We consider ourselves an advanced society, yet within that construct we fail to realize that every single Spark is contributing to our ad-vanced evolution. We must reverse this thinking.

In Chapter Eight, I introduced you to *contrast*, which is our awareness of what we *don't* want. This contrast we create in any given lifetime is necessary to move the needle further and further along, meaning that with each passing millennium, we grow more aware, more curious, and more empowered to understand ourselves. While it may sometimes seem like we're slipping backward as a human race, that contrast we experience does indeed propel us forward, and in fact often ignites latent Sparks just waiting for their moment to burst forth.

A few recent examples of this that come to mind are the murder of George Floyd, the 2020 March on Washington, and the experience our entire planet is undergoing, calling forth the greatness and genius in all of us.

The most significant leaps in human experience have come from people who "thought outside the box" and used their imagination to "see" potentials and realities that were at the time not readily available to the senses. We collectively agree that these individuals are mavericks, that they are unique and special in the world. Yet the reality is this: the only reason we are all not mavericks is because we continue to "drink the Kool-Aid," or rather, believe that we are not also unique and special, or that our imagination only gets us into trouble. How many times have you expressed an innovative idea you hatched in your imagination only to be told, "You're not being realistic!" But, and this is vital: *The only difference between you and being a maverick is your reluctance to break free from the social limitations you have accepted as real, but that are, in fact, nothing more than an illusion.* There is absolutely no reason you can't, like these great innovators, believe in your ability to imagine and then create a new reality, to do the work of building and maintaining your focus. You, too, can believe what you see in your imagination more powerfully than what is presented by your senses. Using your imagination, as you know from reading Chapter Twelve, changes your state of being. It enables you to turn mere thought into something powerful and amazing, and it gives you superhuman ability to see beyond the problems that are typically presented by the five senses. It is within your imagination that your abilities to think and perceive differently blossom. This is precisely why we are continually reminded in our earthly experience to manage our thoughts—because our thoughts become things. Which brings us back to the very nature of God that each of us possesses: desire focused with intention, and then expressed (imagined) in the Universe.

Within the structure of time and space, many of us believe that creation is not simple and certainly not easy. In some regard this is correct—but only because our social training and collective beliefs developed over the millennia of our human existence say it is so, and so we continue to believe it. But your Divine Spark is here to create something only you can. Don't let fear, entrenched in old, misguided beliefs, hold you back from expressing that Spark. Whether you understand it consciously or not, you know at the core of your being that you are a part of something greater—that you are a creator, that you are powerful, that you are in one-ness with God to cultivate that unique Spark that is you.

Have fun with it!

CHAPTER FOURTEEN

Choosing Your Life Path

I n this chapter, I want to help liberate you from fear by asserting something that may ruffle your feathers a bit, particularly if you've been raised in a culture or religion that has an opposing belief—and it is this: we choose our parents. Said another way, and perhaps more correctly, we choose the environment and the energies that will best support the path of exploration we will focus on in a specific lifetime.

I realize this may well be one of the most challenging concepts for you to integrate, but stay with me . . .

At the core of our experience we have free will. We have the freedom to choose everything in our experience—and that means we can also choose bondage. While on a human level it defies logic that we would choose a life that would be rife with pain and struggle, you must remember that we are souls having a human experience, not the other way around. Our human mind cannot necessarily conceive of reasoning that happens on a soul level. But if we look at how "choice" is defined, we can seek to uncover a better understanding of what it means for both a human and a soul.

Typically, when we choose something—anything really—the selection we make is always about outcome. For example: For what reason do you choose what you wear? For what reason do you choose what you eat? For what reason do you choose what you say? The answer is: for the result you think it will create. With clothes it may be being warm, or looking good. For food it may be a craving, or the desire to put nourishing food into your body. Ultimately, the choice is about outcome. Everything else is story created out of an emotional narrative that in some way justifies the reason for the choice.

By the same token, a non-physical being of energy makes choices to simply, and powerfully, create energetic alignments that move and expand its energy to a greater and greater alignment with Love. So, choosing the environment in which we make our big splash into this physical reality would logically seem necessary, right? Now, I can hear you protesting that no soul would choose a horrible environment in order to achieve this alignment with God/Source/Love. And I want to be clear that because you have chosen a certain family does not, in any way, justify their bad behavior or abuse, although these may be a part of the environment. But I also want to make clear that once we are conceived in the physical, we become part of a *co-creative process* because, just as the environment affects us, *we affect the environment we choose.*

As I stated earlier, I know this is a challenging concept, but my hope is that you can begin to understand how it all works toward our soul's evolution. I also want you to internalize how this knowledge has the potential to liberate you from fear.

When you understand that we choose the environment into which we are born, it adds another level of clarity about how dialed in and powerful we are—as beings, as creators, and as the Spark of God. It's crucial to recognize that fear is nowhere in the equation until our focus changes from who we truly are (a soul) to the entrained human we culturally and socially allow ourselves to become. It is that ego-driven, or mass consciousness–driven, being that brings in fear, with all of its belief in unworthiness, separation, and not enough-ness. Although the majority of us will deal with one or more of these unmerited burdens at some point, the power lies in realizing why we are truly here: not to live in a state of fear, but to evolve to the next level in our alignment with Source.

We are all energy, as is everything around us. So, consider that when we are contemplating our new physical life experience, we are contemplating the realization of our potential within the context of time and space, through a physical energetic expression. Our potential is loaded with all the information and energies we have engaged with in previous experiences, both physical and non-physical. This is commonly referred to as karma, which is simply the cause and effect, in energy, that results from *all* of our choices. It is important to grasp that karma is not now, nor never has been, a form of universal punishment. IT IS ALL ABOUT ENERGY.

As we move from experience to experience, or lifetime to lifetime, there is a continual striving for more balance and deeper alignment. In order for that growth and evolution to take place, we must first experience the Law of Cause and Effect, and then, through continuing to choose (consciously or unconsciously), we do whatever is necessary to integrate this understanding. Why is this important? Because it sets the stage for understanding choice, and the responsibility that our freedom to choose carries with it.

There is a great axiom that says, "With great power comes great responsibility." In order to fully grasp this concept of choosing our parents, you must find alignment with this truth. Coming into this life, the creation of Life, is probably the greatest power we can experience in physical form. If you are not created, but are the *creator*, then how could it be any other way? If you are wielding the power of creation, why would you want to believe that any part of your experience is random, or left to chance? The process of being conceived, being born, and experiencing infancy and childhood is all about the integration and transition from non-physical to physical.

Remember, we come here to have an experience, and we choose the environment that best aligns us with our chosen purpose for each experience. ALL of those choices are about exploring, repairing, realigning, integrating, releasing, transforming, connecting, expanding, clarifying, and ultimately, consciously creating your reality.

I want to take a moment here to address this from a parent's perspective. How many times have you heard yourself or someone say, "I will never do to my kids what was done to me?" or "I will do everything the opposite of what my parents did!" or "I don't want to be like my parents." The basis of all these statements is the belief that you were a victim of circumstance. But what if you could understand this: all of your choices have led you to this moment. All of your experiences of love, success, failure, worthiness, power, confusion, abuse, etc., has stimulated all the energies, *in your field*, that you felt were necessary to create your perfect unfolding and growth. All the rest is story that is emotionalized and stored in that field.

If you never come to understand that you chose your parents, you will likely continue to make choices that perpetuate unhealthy generational energies. You will continue to further the illusion of unworthiness and separation in yourself and engender it in your children—and I do not believe any parent wants that. This happens when you simply don't align with the powerful creator that you are, and when you don't honor that in your offspring.

If you are a parent, take this opportunity to internalize that your role is to create the best possible alignment with Love/Source to create the best possible environment, so that this new, precious being can assimilate into his or her new environment. And whether you're a parent or not, be liberated in your knowing that you can choose to be a victim of your circumstances, or you can realize you've been be a co-creator in your life all along. If your choice is alignment with your Self, your path becomes inspired, and your choices will be born out of that inspiration.

CHAPTER FIFTEEN

You Don't HAVE to Align,
You GET to Align

When I was diagnosed with cancer, I had to, among other things, take a long look at what I had been aligning with in my life that was separating me from Source. Was it insecurity or resentment? Anger or old emotional wounds? Sadness or regret? Because as hard as it was to comes to terms with, I had to own that I had—on an energetic level—welcomed that dis-ease into my body.

I realize this may be a tough concept to swallow; many of us would much rather blame the seeming maladies that occur in our lives on outside influences. But the truth is, whatever we are in alignment with determines what we are choosing—and we do indeed choose everything we have. The same way we choose our parents and the environment that will best help us to evolve when we come into this human body, we also choose the thoughts, feelings, and actions that consciously, or unconsciously, create the events and circumstances of our lives. This occurs through a multitude of decisions we make on a daily basis—how we feel about ourselves, how we feel about others, how we view the world, what we believe, etc.—and making those our consistent offering at a vibrational level. And all of this stems from how aligned, or misaligned, we choose to be with God/Source.

In my case, one of the most startling revelations that occurred after I was diagnosed with cancer was the realization that my marriage, once connected and powerful, had become seriously diminished. We were no longer creating powerful transformational and healing processes and modalities as we had for many years. Our energies together—and my energy in particular—had seemingly devolved into a morass of negative, combative, ugly vibrations that ultimately created lots of little black clouds wherever we went. I had reached a point where I didn't care where we were or what we were doing; if I perceived her coming for me, judging me, attacking me, or any number of other excuses, I would lose my shit. It didn't matter if we were home, at a restaurant, in a store, or in the car. The slightest perception of provocation sent me over the edge. I would yell, curse, attack—whatever would (hopefully) create impact. My personal pain was off the charts, as was my judgment of myself and my spouse.

But here is where the rubber met the road. I was hiding, and I was using my spouse as an energetic punching bag, somehow deciding that she was the reason for my unhappiness, when I was really fighting myself over my lack of authenticity, my lack of *alignment* with Self.

You see, I am, and was, a gay man. My wife knew that when I met her, she knew my history, and she chose to be with me for twenty-four years anyway. I realize some people may not understand why we entered into such an unconventional partnership, but for us, it was about having a deep sense of connection and purpose in our energy together. We loved each other deeply, and I chose to take my focus off being a gay man, which for me, to that point, was all about sex—the more the merrier. I needed to focus on finding out who I was as a man, and I *consciously* chose to focus differently. To be clear, my sexuality never changed, but it definitely expanded, and it had to be a regular part of our ongoing conversations because it was always there. It wasn't until those final years together that I struggled to keep that focus, when it became abundantly clear that I was not allowing my most authentic expression to shine through. In short, I was no longer able to NOT live as a gay man. Because I had grown so profoundly during my marriage, I could no longer maintain the separation within myself.

I realized, sitting in the parking lot that day after leaving the doctor's office, that I had been in fear for a long time. I was afraid I would die if I allowed myself to align with my authentic Self and live in that truth. I feared "being okay" in the world without my wife. I also feared my own energy because, for too long, I had allowed myself to indulge in deep negativity. It was also in that moment that I "saw" with absolute clarity how all of my choices had led me to that moment, and that I now had a huge choice to make: either step up and into my Truth, walk it in integrity, and course correct so that both of us could release these horrible energies we had embraced—or continue to blame her and all the crap I had made up. In the end, it was absolutely clear that it was time to surrender it all and step into this powerful new clarity.

For me, in that moment, I finally understood that what I had been doing was wholly inadequate and not in keeping with what I knew in my heart. It was also not what I had worked so hard to learn and process about myself, my energy, and my life. The choice was clear and obvious because I chose surrender. I chose to stop fighting and resisting. Instead, I chose Self. And when I did, the clarity I experienced was visceral—I experienced it with every cell of my body. The uplifting of my being was something I could not ignore, or turn my back on. In effect, stepping into alignment with Self became a choiceless choice. Even though I had no idea what would come next, I experienced a clarity that only comes when we lose all resistance and allow truth to flood through us.

That was the moment I no longer aligned with fear.

As you already know from reading this book, aligning with fear is the default for many people because we have been trained into fear in three prevalent ways.

The first is that we buy into the collective belief that fear is an intrinsic part of our experience. We are taught that we humans came into existence wired that way. And while of course we did come here wired for survival, it does not mean we are wired to be fearful.

The second is through the persistent belief that we are separate from God. In internalizing this belief, the world becomes a scary and unsafe place to be. If we view multiple things as a threat, it's difficult not to assign fear to multiple aspects of our lives.

And the third is the assumption that everything (or most everything) happens *to* us, without us having much say in it. This causes people to expect the next bad thing to happen, which can place people in perpetual fear.

Even the concept of alignment itself has been turned into a job. If you've ever heard that you're responsible to do "the work" to figure out how to get into alignment, you may believe that it is indeed your job to learn how to "Be." But how do you work at being what you already are, which is the evolution of God expressed as matter? That would be like a baby tiger thinking it is a human baby, fighting and resisting itself because it cannot walk on two legs, or because it cannot speak. Even this example doesn't make sense!

But once you realize that feelings of inadequacy, unworthiness, brokenness, or a belief in your "lack of" all arise from within the consciousness of fear, you can then see clearly that none of these concepts or beliefs are created or born out of what we all truly are—which is God, or in complete one-ness with God. And this is when choosing your alignment becomes such a joy. Why? *Be-*

cause alignment with the reality of who you are means accepting that you are not an inherently fearful being. You may be choosing to experience life one way—as fear—but you can choose to experience it another way, as God. We could get into a lengthy dialogue here about ego, but that is for another time. For now, what is important to know regarding negative ego is that it cannot be present when aligned with the energy of God, which is Love. So why do we *get* to align instead of *have* to?

By its very nature, alignment speaks to all aspects holding the same perspective. In fact, it is defined as "a position of agreement or alliance," which means all parties are free to choose their position. In this case it is God, Higher Self, and human being—the true trinity of power. And when you understand that the only part of this trinity that can move out of the synergistic union is the human being, you realize just how empowered you are to choose. In other words, God and your Higher Self never choose to be out of alignment with you; only you as a human being can step out of alignment from "them."

Let's examine this a bit closer. God and our Higher Self express a consistent vibration and energy that creates a space or state of Love. But, as humans entrained in fear, we tend to push against, fight, battle, work, struggle, and generally disturb our experience to varying degrees in our attempts to find purpose, freedom, and Love. And the only reason we are searching so desperately is because we exist in our own created illusion of unworthiness. There are as many varieties of this illusion as there are people and the thoughts created, because fear can be so beguiling and compelling that it consumes our focus and attention.

But, getting into alignment is simply allowing and yielding to what is the core of who we are: the Soul, the Essence. It is not work. It is simply where we put our attention.

A telling example of this lies in the biblical story about Sodom and Gomorrah. In the story, Lot and his wife are instructed to leave the city and to not look back as the sins of the past are destroyed (which, in this case, is symbolized by the destruction of the city and all the people in it). Lot continues looking forward, but his wife yields to the temptation, and in looking back is instantly turned into a pillar of salt. The metaphor illustrates that by looking backward, we align with our own destruction. Instead of being in the moment and looking forward toward what *can* be, our attachment to things of the past, our turning back to what *was*, can be our undoing. In this parable, Lot's wife becoming a pillar of salt shows that she lost her very humanity, her being.

Now, this does not mean that we should never reflect or engage in fond memories. The message here is that when we look backward—either in regret, in wishing something could have been different, or in trying to understand or define "meaning" in our present situation or experience, all of which stem from some level of fear— the only thing we accomplish is the re-engagement of old energy. In other words, when our alignment is fear (the opposite of alignment with God/Source), we tend to continually look back so we can remember why we are afraid, and this is certainly not the alignment we want to choose. Our journey is ever forward, and evolution only moves in that direction.

This is why it's incredibly empowering and delight-ful to know that we *get* to align—that every time we choose our alignment with who we truly are, God and Love, we cut the ties and release the hooks created by our misalignment with fear. Once we are able to consistently choose this healthy and joyful new alignment, it will shift into becoming our way of Being, and those ties and hooks to fear will exist no more.

CHAPTER SIXTEEN

Taking a Leap of Faith

We have all heard stories about people who "took a leap of faith" in order to make a quantum leap from where they were in their lives, to a place where they felt their passion explode. I am one of those people, and this is how it happened...

Back in the spring of 2012, I was working in the restaurant industry as a manager. I was deeply distressed with my work, the industry I was in, and the future I felt it had for me. I had spent over twenty years of my life in the industry, and I was extremely good at what I did, but I disliked getting up for it every day. I did everything I could think of to vent these negative feelings, including wearing out my good friends with my upset, drama, frustration, and emotional turmoil, but the bottom line was that I was so deeply dissatisfied, I felt I had truly reached an impasse. However, not being in a position to just up and quit, I worked diligently to get aligned with what I was doing.

As I consciously focused on shifting the negative feelings I was having, I was able to see clearly that my issues had *nothing* to do with the company, or with the people I worked with and for. In contrast, I was feeling a deep and powerful pull toward something that was not clear to me, as if the unrelenting feeling of dissatisfaction wasn't about forcing alignment with my current job, but rather pushing me to make a change. Despite speaking with my boss and discussing alternatives within the company, the feelings would not yield. I simply couldn't see a future for myself there. I only saw a trajectory of "same/same."

The breaking point finally came in a kind of surprising way.

I had been introduced to the concept of appreciation by a good friend. She described this process of consciously and actively appreciating, out loud, anything and everything I could think of, about every detail in my life, the way I illustrated for you with the bathroom example back in Chapter Six. It was quite an awkward process in the beginning. But I continued to stumble my way through, and in short order, it became my twice daily exercise. I would do my "rampage of appreciation" in the car on the ten- to fifteen-minute drive to and from work, which was a perfect amount of time to focus my attention.

One day, shortly after incorporating this new ritual, I had just finished my day and was in the car driving home. I took a deep breath and started my appreciation process. As I dove in to this practice of giving thanks, I heard myself say, "I appreciate that I made it through today." SCREEEECH!!!! What?!?! I appreciate that I made it through the day? WTF? I quickly realized that I had said the exact same thing the past three days in a row. While I was glad I could appreciate it, I was definitely not okay with the idea of my life being about "just getting through it." In that moment, I knew it was time to leap.

It was the beginning of May when I recognized that regardless of anything else going on in my life, I could no longer continue to do the same type of work I was doing, or even remain in the restaurant industry. The time had come for me to take a leap of faith, which meant leaving everything that provided my physical security to pursue a new security, a new way of being. My clarity with my choice astounded me; it was unwavering and powerful.

My next step was to discuss my decision with my spouse. Luckily, I was not the least bit concerned. I knew he would understand because he truly gets me and is incredibly supportive. In fact, I wasn't going into the conversation seeking permission. I simply wanted to share my new aligned reality with him to make sure we were on the same page. So we gathered for a "powwow," which is what we call coming together to connect and talk about important stuff. Our process is to create a sacred space between us where we start with our love for each other and then dive into whatever either of us needs to talk about. (It's an amazing and powerful technique, by the way.)

So we sat on the bed and held hands. I dove in, sharing all that had unfolded, and what my choice and next step was going to be.

Immediately coming off the rails, he said, "Are you nuts?! You're going to leave your job with no backup? No plan?!"

I had not seen this coming, and I instantly responded defensively. The ensuing argument resulted in a state of mutual turmoil that lasted for three days.

During that time, I kept ruminating on how blown away and disappointed I was by his response. I even lamented about it to other family members, but they, too, recommended I take a more conservative route by finding another position within the company, or hold on until I found something else. Interestingly, though, neither my spouse's nor my family's responses swayed me. My feeling of clarity was so profound, I knew that even if my husband walked away from our relationship, I would still move forward because I *had* to.

As I imagined not only leaving my job, but also the industry—for good—I was bolstered by amazing support from God and the Universe. I felt ready. I felt ALIVE. All in all, it felt undeniably right.

So, after completing my due diligence, I took the leap.

In brief, I stopped working "for the man." I started my own coaching company, Got Joy, and began hosting twice weekly meetups and seminars.

Just as expected, it has been nothing short of IN-CREDIBLE, AMAZING, AWESOME, and filled with JOY. I won't pretend that the leap and the journey were not a little scary in the beginning. But what I discovered was that taking a leap of faith was really about trusting myself completely, and knowing that God/Universe has my back. In that process, I reached a deep, visceral knowing that I was well and taken care of at all times. I also felt a deep sense of relief coupled with a profound sense of alignment. It was and continues to be exhilarating, powerful, and transformative.

I should mention here that while I was rich in my convictions, I wasn't so rich elsewhere. I left my restaurant career with no money in the bank, no savings, no backup plan, and no fallback position. But what I *did* have was a powerful FAITH and TRUST in myself that I was pursuing the path that was right for me, a path that has filled me with aliveness and brought me more joy than I could have ever believed. In short, I found clarity about my life experience that radically altered my being.

I share this with you as a loving reminder that sometimes we all need our own "leap of faith" to remember who we are—and why we are here. If you're feeling misaligned in your career, job, relationship, spiritual path—anything at all—and the signs have been nudging you in another direction, know that is happening for a REASON. You, as each of us on this planet, have extraordinary gifts to contribute, and you have so much more to give *yourself* than you have likely been giving. This life is about YOUR experience, YOUR aliveness, YOUR growth, YOUR joy. If the circumstances of your life aren't satisfying these experiences, maybe it is time for you to think about the "leap" you can take to find your alignment.

Before you freak out like my spouse did, remember

that leaps come in all shapes and sizes. Do not think you have to turn your life upside down or lay waste to everything you know. Start by getting quiet and centered, and then engaging your clarity. You do that by finding that place that is *your* joy. What would excite you to jump out of bed and do each day? What dormant creativity is waiting to blossom? What dreams have you put aside because your egoic mind or someone else told you they weren't feasible?

At this point in the clarity-reaching process, it is not about knowing where your new destination is, although you may have some ideas about that. It is about recognizing that where you currently are is not in the greater alignment you are yearning for. The desire to leap comes when you recognize this. The yearning for that greater alignment explodes your potential for a bigger, better, and more expanded, powerful, and satisfying experience. By deciding to take the leap, you allow yourself to go in search of where your happiness truly resides. Why is this important? Because you are *meant* to be happy. Let go, right now, of any old story you've been telling yourself that you don't deserve happiness. Whatever you may have done in the past that you feel regret about, or whatever criticism you've placed on yourself about where you are versus where you think you should be, *let it go*. This is the most important part of building faith and trust in yourself, and breaking free of fear.

Next, trust enough to allow yourself to take the first tiny leap. By starting small, you will be able to build faith and trust in yourself. Know in your heart that pursuing that which brings you joy will fill you in ways you cannot yet imagine. And remember that trusting in yourself means you may have no idea *how* things will unfold; the *how* is not important. By keeping your focus on what you want, and how you want to feel, your focus will remain fixed on moving forward, not on *how* to move forward. When you maintain this forward focus, you build faith as your awareness and consciousness are focused in potential and opportunity. This means you are aware and present, which in turn allows you to witness your unfolding. Each minuscule leap of faith builds momentum in the direction you want to go. But keep in mind, as we discussed in the previous chapter, that if you are looking back (in history) for meaning, you will stay rooted in your old beliefs. History can only repeat itself it you choose to live there. This is how fear works. It keeps you looking back at what *was* and hoping that it will not be what *is*. This is the opposite of forward focus.

I'll leave you with the best entreaty I know for taking a leap of faith.

When you fully embrace trust, you can be certain that everything you have done in your life thus far has prepared you for where you are going. Trust allows you to live in anticipation of realizing your greatness. It is leaping into all that you are with the clarity that fear has no place in your reality because it cannot exist where it is not allowed. It is understanding that fear is an illusion created to keep you in sameness, to keep you safe on the treadmill of other's expectations, whereas trust allows you to take responsibility for your *own* expectations. And, perhaps most importantly, when you are serving your inner voice and moving toward all of your potential, in alignment and with focus and intention, you will always be caught when you take the leap.

CHAPTER SEVENTEEN

The Joy Really IS in the Journey

We have arrived at the final chapter, and the final message I have for you with regard to living in liberation from fear, and that is that the joy really *is* in the journey. Let me illustrate an example of this by sharing a personal story.

I like to hike a mountain trail very near to where I live. It is a moderate trail, but strenuous, and provides great exercise. It is also absolutely beautiful and does not take long to reach places that offer breathtaking views. On this particular day, I was consciously appreciative of how close the trail is to my home and how much I love mountains, dirt, rocks, and being in nature. I did a little stretching to warm up, then started off at a good clip, setting a pace I felt confident I could maintain. I focused on a three-foot-square area in front of me to ensure my safety, and I was mindful of my breathing. As my respiration rate increased, I could feel my breaths more deeply in my chest, which I knew was my healthy body responding to the inflow of oxygen. At a certain point, however, I noticed a tingly, itchy feeling in my head, which I have come to associate with intense exertion. At the same time, I was completely focused on my destination: making it to the top of the mountain for the first time. As I climbed higher and strove to maintain my pace, I found it more difficult to satisfy my body's demands for increased oxygen.

About a third of the way up the mountain, I realized I would not be making it to the top. It had been a while since I had done this type of hike, or exerted myself this strongly, and I was feeling the strain through my entire body. When I checked in with my body, I knew that pushing forward did not feel good, and that I could not sustain the strenuous pace I had set. So when I came to a level part of the trail, I decided to stop. My first thought was that I would rest just long enough to catch my breath, give my body a little break, and then carry on, heeding that part of my mind telling me to push, push, push forward to make it to the top. As in so many other areas of life, we often force ourselves to reach whatever destination we have set our minds on, even if a little voice is telling us we are no longer aligned with it. In my case, my mind was working overtime to convince me that my body would be fine if I just gave it a brief rest.

As I paced back and forth, I took a sip of water and looked up the mountain. Certainly it seemed achievable; I could see lots of people climbing near the top. Then I gazed out at the scenery from my vantage point. Even though I had only made it about a third of the way, from where I was I could see up and down the entire coast of southern California, from La Jolla to Tijuana, Mexico. It was a remarkable sight on this clear, beautiful day.

Taking in the view, I had a brief conversation with my body, hoping it would tell me it was ready to power up the rest of the mountain so I could take in the 360-degree view from the top. But my body said "no." Thankfully, I recognized this clarity of connection with my body from the inside rather than from the willful mind. I knew I had the energy to get back down the mountain safely—but *only* if I turned back from this point.

My mind kept pestering me, though. As my body relaxed a bit from stopping, I found myself reasoning that I could push through whatever pain or discomfort might develop and began to move in the direction of "up." But I distinctly felt my body telling me *no* yet again. So, against my logical judgment, I decided to yield to my body's needs and return to the bottom.

The more relaxed movement and gravitational momentum of descending a trail always becomes a fun game to navigate the trail, the rocks, and the people going past, and I focused once again on the three-foot square in front of me until I arrived safely at the bottom. My legs felt like Jell-O, so I continued to walk leisurely, allowing my body to cool down. It was during this period that I become deeply aware of what I had just experienced: it was truly one of those moments where the microcosm—smaller parts of the whole, and the macrocosm—the whole of the universe, came together in the same moment, a moment of clarity so profound it could not be missed.

Before we get to that amazing revelation, however, you're probably wondering what this story has to do with living in liberation from fear.

Initially, my reason for going on the hike was to move my energy and give my body a workout. But shortly after arriving, my *mind* (ego) decided that summiting the mountain was a good idea, although reaching the top was not *my* intended "destination." This is where fear could have played a role, but didn't. First, on a primitive level, because I hadn't hiked for a while, I could have let fear keep me from even trying to accomplish something so ambitious as reaching the top. But I didn't. Next, on a bit higher level, when I began to realize I couldn't make it as far as I planned, I could have let fear energy (disguised as anger, frustration, and disappointment) turn me quickly around and miss the view altogether. But instead, as we've talked about extensively in this book, I recognized that the voice was merely my internal guidance system—a voice very different from my ego/*fear* voice— gently nudging me toward being present without thought of the original goal: summiting the mountain. As a result, that experience of presence was heightened after I made it back down, where a subsequent moment of clarity led to the delivery of a profound message:

> **When we choose to focus solely on the destination, we become so destination-oriented that we forget about the meaning of the journey.**

When this message came to me, it solidified not only how myopic I had become when I latched on to my summiting goal, but also how many times I had missed the meaning of my journeys because I had let the illusion of fear hijack me. I realized that in the same way our Emotional Guidance System "speaks" to us to let us know when we are out of alignment with our purpose—with Source—which gives us that feeling of uneasiness that many of us wrongly interpret as fear, it is also frequently giving us clues that may look like "failure" or something going "wrong" that in reality are protecting us, redirecting us, or giving us an opportunity to glean something of incredible value.

On that particular day, my body's exhaustion was offering me all three: I was protected from getting injured, or even stranded higher up; I was redirected to stop and take in the breathtaking view where I was; and I was gifted with a profound moment of clarity when I reached the bottom that likely wouldn't have occurred otherwise, at least not on that day.

For many years, I assumed that the saying "the joy is in the journey" was nothing more than a sweet idea created to help people find solace within an experience when things didn't "appear" to be going the right way. But in that moment, I realized just how off the mark I had been.

Yes, it is necessary and important to have a destination in mind with most everything you do. But at the same time, there is no requirement that the "destination" be a place or an accomplishment or an achievement. The destination can also be a feeling, or an experience, or a moment. As a person becomes more and more conscious, the desired destination becomes less a tangible achievement and more a place of desired *feeling*, and it is from this achievement of feeling that all experiences come.

Had I allowed fear to turn me quickly around and race back to the bottom of that mountain, or internalized a sense of "failure" to make me think not making it to the top rendered the entire trek useless, I would have had no chance to take in what the Universe was trying to show me.

Think about it: if you are solely focused on the tangible part of your destination, you greatly limit what and how much you experience because your focus is narrowed. When I was hiking, limiting my view to a three-foot-square space in front of me meant that I missed a great deal of what was so amazing and beautiful around me. With my view of navigating the quickest, most efficient way to get to my desired destination, I was so focused on getting to the top of the mountain that I failed to really notice the people flowing past me. I was also breathing so hard that I wasn't able to appreciate the smells of the blooming plants and flowers. I was missing some truly awe-inspiring, life-affirming parts of the trail and the hiking experience because I was determined to get to *the* view—the one at the top.

If you've thought, at one time or another, *Why would I want anything less than the ultimate view? Why waste my time on the small stuff along the way?*

Well, here's why.

Because all of my resources (physical, emotional, mental, and spiritual) were intensely focused on achieving my goal of reaching the top, I had left no room to appreciate my body's agility, take in the view along the way, or notice the subtle changes of mother nature. I didn't consider how far I had come, or what I had accomplished to reach the spot where I stopped, a place that offered amazing joy. I didn't take any time to enjoy the people who were near me on their own journey, or even to say hello. And, had I pushed myself to struggle my way to the top, I would have been so depleted when I arrived that relishing the glory of the views would have likely been eclipsed by my exhaustion. When you look at my hike this way, there seems to be very little enjoyment at all!

Another example would be planning a road trip from the West Coast to the East Coast, then back home. Ultimately, you'll end up back home on the West Coast, right? So, taking the "destination matters most" perspective, why bother going at all? You might as well stay on the West Coast!

Yet another would be becoming a parent, with the sole intention of getting that child to adulthood, nose to the grindstone the whole way through, your sights set on nothing but that child's eighteenth birthday when you can send him or her off into the world.

These examples may seem exaggerated, but I offer them to make a point.

It is crucial that we understand how the journey itself often has so much more to offer us even than reaching our destination. Whether it's a road trip, a work project, raising a child, or a hike in nature, what occurs along the way is all part of what makes the goal itself meaningful. In the road trip example, you wouldn't just blaze through all the states without enjoying the scenery, the landmarks, or the other fun experiences a planned road trip offers to get to the opposite coast, would you? Of course not. The whole point of the road trip would be all the fun and learning opportunities you would have along the way. The same is true with most any start-to-finish plan. (Okay, so you may have a hard time finding the "joy in the journey" cleaning the toilet, but even that can have its feelings of gratification as you go!)

It is said by many masters and great teachers that our life experience is merely a reflection of consciousness—that even the smallest things are reflective of much bigger things, and that these smaller things assist us to awaken to greater and greater realities in consciousness. Indeed, when we step back to observe our experiences, we can frequently see how one event connects to another, and then another, to bring us to a specific point in life—a job opportunity, a relationship, a meaningful connection, a home, a friendship, an understanding, an elevation of the soul, the list goes on.

We so often forget, in our microcosm focus, that we are so much more than this little human body. That's because our ability as humans to imagine the big picture pales in comparison to God's big-picture perspective about our human experience. In other words, from this Divine viewpoint, all of our fulfillment, joy, peace, love, growth, wisdom, expansion, and *destination* as humans actually comes from the journey itself. Yes . . . another paradox!

This is why I want to encourage you to think twice about your tendency to bust your butt and "grind out" whatever it is you're trying to achieve. It may be admirable to maintain powerful focus and intense drive to get to your destination, but when you arrive, you may find it somewhat lacking. The view might still be remarkable, but your resources will possibly be so depleted that you cannot fully enjoy and embrace where you've landed. In other words, by focusing so intently on the microcosm of life, you end up not being present in very few, if any, moments along the way.

Think about that in relation to yourself and how you tend to go through life. Are you a "head down and grind it out" type? Are you a list maker who is so focused on the checkmark next to each item you finish that you forget to enjoy the tasks themselves? Or are you a savorer of life who actually takes the time to be fully present for each segment of your day?

At this point, I'm sure it's sinking in that the latter—when you take the time and energy to enjoy and engage the journey—the entire experience not only becomes one of magic and adventure, but it also feeds and fills you. You are able to experience yourself in connection with all that is around you, and you are aware *in* the moments and *of* the moments. On a hike, this awareness translates to recognizing the amazing smells, viewing the ever-changing panoramas, allowing the body to acclimate and adjust so it can continue, drinking water and feeling it nourish the body, calming the breath, hearing the nature sounds, etc. During a normal workday, the awareness may translate to nourishing yourself with a good break-fast; enjoying the ride to work with a great podcast, music, or audiobook; using your gifts or skills to uncover a help-ful solution or embark on a creative project; engaging positively with coworkers; bringing a new idea to a meeting, etc.

No matter what the endeavor, savoring the journey is about being in as many moments as possible so that upon reaching the end goal of the destination—even if it's something as simple as going from home to work, or from the start of your day to the end of it—you are fully present in that experience, as you had been throughout. Can you see how operating this way brings so much more to that moment and to that experience?

When we don't give that to ourselves—particularly for bigger undertakings, such as career-related moves, radical athletic endeavors, building a house, becoming a parent, and the like—it can be easy to feel disappoint-ment and discouragement, and maybe even disillusion-ment, by what we find at the destination. This occurs because frequently, we forget or neglect to include *our-selves* as a part of that destination. What that means is that the idea of the destination may have sounded so good to you that you didn't stop to think about how *you* would experience it yourself. You may have, erroneously, assumed that your experience reaching this destination would mirror the experience of another person who "got there," or deliver the same satisfaction you read or heard about, or saw on TV, which is quite often not the case. Your journeys and destinations are unique to *you*; they can never reflect or mirror what was achieved by another person, even on a similar path, and the steps of any journey you travel—within a single day, within months, within years, and even within the span of your lifetime—exist to prepare you for each level of awareness and connection to the Divine you are here to achieve.

The bottom line is, on any journey we pick up pieces of ourselves, pieces that will play an important role in how deeply we enjoy the destination once we get there. I believe that we oftentimes, metaphorically, drive like crazy to get to our destination because we think it will not be there for us if we don't hurry. But what's vital for us to realize is that this viewpoint of potential loss comes from a consciousness of *lack*. This is found in the school of human thought that says "there is only so much to go around, so I had better get mine before someone else gets it." Yet the truth is actually the exact opposite. All of the connections, serendipities, coincidences, and inspirations we need to get to our destination show up in the journey. They are found in those moments of intense appreciation for all the amazing things that *can* and *do* happen when we focus our attention on what's occurring on our way to the end goal.

Circling back to my hiking analogy, which can be applied to anything we do in life with merely a few tweaks to the details, I now view my hikes as joy-filled adventures that expand my experience, allowing me to explore more and work my way to the top. I savor the smells, the sights, the sounds, the view. I listen to my body. I work to expand my potential with each step. I smile, I breathe mindfully and fully, and most importantly, I appreciate where I am, recognize that fear has no place in my journey, and anticipate the joy of reaching my destination. And because of the richness of my path, the destination is no longer the end, but rather a stop along the journey to the next point in my evolution.

Your life is no different.

ACKNOWLEDGMENTS

I have always felt "connected" in my life. For as far back as I can remember, I never felt alone. But to be clearer, I always felt a special relationship with God. That led me to be curious and very open to exploring non-traditional ideas of God and the Universe. Everything for me has always been driven by deep feeling and an innate understanding of energy and how it works, feels, interacts, expresses, and so on. When I say everything, I truly mean *everything*. The more I've explored my path, my energy, my consciousness, and my existence, the more I've been led to circumstances, people, teachings, and experiences that fueled my awakening and growth. My process has been very monk-like, yet I've chosen to navigate my unfolding fully engaged in the world, as opposed to withdrawing from it.

I offer deep appreciation for the following influences:

The first two books I clearly remember as pivotal for me were, *I Come As a Brother* by Bartholomew, and *What Ever Happened to Divine Grace?* by Ramon Stevens. Both had a profound impact because they were the first books I encountered that spoke about my experience of life within the context of consciousness and energy. I was also influenced by *A Treatise on White Magic* by Alice A. Bailey. When I first started it twenty-five years ago, I wasn't ready for the level of wisdom it imparted, and it put me to sleep! Flash forward twenty-five years, however, and I experienced tears streaming down my face at the depth of clarity and information I took in from her words.

Continually expanding my understanding of the soul, energy, and higher consciousness has become a life-long pattern for me, one that I cherish because of the amazing validation it has brought to my experiences. Reading books, meeting people, or having conversations where I've learned that what I previously experienced actually had a name, or was part of an entire teaching I hadn't known about, has been remarkable. My sincere thanks to Mona, my teacher, my guide, my wife. You have been my greatest influence, guiding me through the darkest aspects of my self and teaching me how to Be. Barbara, thank you for catapulting me into the work that would lead me to my greatest expansion and revelation, setting me up for amazing success and incredible growth. Jayne, thank you for believing in me, truly seeing me, and uplifting me. Selina and Paul, thank you for introducing me to parts of myself, and to my power that had been locked away for a long time. I am deeply grateful that you were with me every step through my Kundalini awakening, holding space, grounding energy, and navigating my unfolding. Tamar, thank you for the countless hours of time, love, and most importantly encouragement you gave to helping me mold the words in this book. And to my mom, thank you for providing just enough Earth energy, Love, and logic to enable me to feel my way into my life and still maintain balance, ask questions, and not accept incongruent energy.

I've participated in some powerful workshops and programs, and have been profoundly influenced by amazing teachers like Mike Dooley and Esther Hicks. Their books and seminars have had a measurable impact on my continued awakening, continually helping me to fill in the pieces and gain increasing clarity and understanding. Other works of great influence came from writers like Dan Millman, Dr. Daniel Amen, Wayne Dyer, Yogananda, and others of note. But perhaps the most explosive and quantum experience of transformation came through Higher Brain Living. This work by Michael Cotton became the foundation from which my life work grew and expanded.

Another deep source of inspiration came from building, living, and working in a residential natural healing center in Arizona for many years as the Director of Aliveness. My wife at the time—a shaman, trained by the Hopi —was the genius of the center and an amazing channel and teacher. Together we designed short- and long-term programs that brought people from all over the world who were seeking natural alternatives to treating disease. We helped people with everything from AIDS, cancer, lupus, and MS, to cleansing and personal development work. In a week-long seminar we called the Power Intensive, we addressed the physical, emotional, mental, and spiritual areas of the participants' lives. I also conducted the physical therapy aspects of treatment, which included massage, energy work, trigger points, crystal and music therapy, and field trips to the Grand Canyon with clients to reintroduce them to their aliveness. These people came for their own healing, but they became some of my greatest teachers.

Along with the residents of our healing center, I have had amazing mentors and teachers—formidable people of integrity who showed up at different junctures in my life to facilitate quantum growth and development, particularly with regard to the core understanding that every response to life comes from only two sources: Love or fear.

And last, but certainly not least, my greatest support—through my awakening, my crazies, my writing, my many almost unbelievable hoops I put him through—is my husband Michael. He has taught me so much about what unconditional means. He has uplifted me, loved me, and believed in me—at times more than I did in myself. His love has known no bounds or conditions. The depth of my love and appreciation for you is immeasurable.

RECOMMENDED READING

Bach, Richard. *Illusions: The Adventures of a Reluctant Messiah*. Eastbourne, UK: Gardners Books, Reprint edition, 2001.

Bach, Richard. *Jonathan Livingston Seagull: A Story*. New York: Avon, First Paperback Printing edition, 1973.

Bach, Richard. *One: A Novel*. New York: Dell, Reissue edition, 1989.

Bailey, Alice A. *A Treatise on White Magic*. New York: Lucis Publishing Company, 2nd edition, 1998.

———*Esoteric Psychology, Vol 1: A Treatise on the Seven Rays*. New York: Lucis Publishing Company, reprint edition, 1971.

Bartholomew, Mary-Margaret Moore, Joy Franklin, and Jill Kramer. *I Come As a Brother: A Remembrance of Illusion*. New York: Hay House Inc, 1997.

Benner, Joseph S. *The Impersonal Life*. Rhode Island: Sun Publishing, 1941.

Byrne, Rhonda. *The Secret*. New York: Simon & Schuster, UK, 2006.

Castaneda, Carlos. *Journey to Ixtlan: The Lessons of Don Juan*. New York: Washington Square Press, Original ed. Edition, 1991.

———*Separate Reality: Conversations with Don Juan*. New York: Washington Square Press, Original ed. Edition, 1991.

——*The Teachings of Don Juan: A Yaqui Way of Knowledge.* New York: Washington Square Press, Reissue edition, 1985.

Cope, Stephen. *The Greatest Work of Your Life.* New York: Bantam Books, 2012.

Costa, Rebecca D. *The Watchman's Rattle.* New York: Vanguard Press, 2010.

Dooley, Mike. *Infinite Possibilities: The Art of Living Your Dreams.* New York: Atria Books/Beyond Words, 2009.

——*Leveraging the Universe: 7 Steps to Engaging Life's Magic.* New York: Atria Books/Beyond Words, Reprint edition, 2012.

——*Manifesting Change: It Couldn't Be Easier.* New York: Atria Books/Beyond Words, 1st edition, 2010.

Dyer, Wayne. *Secret Fulfilled: Mastering the Art of Manifesting.* New York: Hay House Inc., 2012.

——*The Power of Intention.* New York: Hay House Inc., 1st edition, 2006.

Hess, Hermann. *Siddhartha.* Lits, 2010.

Hicks, Esther, and Jerry Hicks. *The Law of Attraction: The Basics of the Teachings of Abraham.* New York: Hay House Inc., 1st edition, 2006.

Lambrick, Dana. *Insight Is 20/20.* New Falcon Press, 2003.

Lipton, Bruce H. *The Biology of Belief.* New York: Hay House, 2005.

Millman, Dan. *Way of the Peaceful Warrior: A Book That Changes Lives.* H.J. Kramer, 2006.

Quinn, Daniel. *Ishmael.* New York: Bantam Books, 1992.

Ramtha, and Steven L. Weinberg. *Ramtha: An Introduction.* Sovereignty Press, 1988.

Rand, Ayn, and Leonard Peikoff. *The Fountainhead.* New York: Signet, 1996.

——*Atlas Shrugged.* New York: Signet, 1996.

Roberts, Jane. *Seth Speaks.* New York: Bantam, 1984.

——*The Nature of Personal Reality, Practical Techniques for Solving Everyday Problems and Enriching the Life You Know.* Amber-Allen Publ., New World Library, Reprint edition, 1994.

Shin, Florence Scovel. *The Writings of Florence Scovel-Shin.* Camarillo, CA: DeVorss & Company, 1988.

Singer, Michael A. *The Untethered Soul.* Oakland, CA: New Harbinger Publications, 2007.

Stevens, Ramon. *What Ever Happened to Divine Grace?* New York: EP Dutton, 1988.

Wilber, Ken. *The Integral Vision.* New York: Shambhala Publishing, 2007.

Yogananda, Paramahansa. *Autobiography of a Yogi.* Yogananda Fellowship, 1946.

R. James Case ("Jim") is passionate about assisting people to achieve the quantum shift and change they desire. He has worked for three decades to impact the spiritual and growth communities, beginning with being the Aliveness Coach for an all-natural residential healing center in Arizona. Here, he developed programs, conducted transformational seminars, and offered one-on-one coaching and aliveness therapy for people confronting terminal and non-terminal disease processes. Jim has also worked with hundreds of clients across the country with his program "The Science of Transformation." He is currently the host of the Live Show and podcast, Adventures in Truth.

Jim has been married to his husband Michael for ten years. They are avid adventurers, traveling and taking road trips regularly, and have recently relocated from San Diego, CA, to Denver, CO.

Fear Is a Choice is his first book.

www.adventuresintruth.com

CPSIA information can be obtained
at www.ICGtesting.com
Printed in the USA
LVHW031152230920
666817LV00006B/535

9 781735 213606